The Vision of James

Stephen C. Rowe gained his M.Th., A.M. and Ph.D. from the Divinity School, University of Chicago. He has studied and taught philosophy and religion for more than twenty-five years and at present is Professor and Chair of Philosophy at Grand Valley State University, Allendale, Michigan. As well as his numerous contributions to periodicals, his publications include *Leaving and Returning, Claiming a Liberal Education* and *Rediscovering the West*. He is also co-ordinator of the Liberal Studies Program at GVSU.

Martin E. Marty is Fairfax M. Cone Distinguished Service Professor of the History of Modern Christianity at the University of Chicago. He is Senior Editor of *The Christian Century* and the author of numerous books including *A Nation of Behavers* and *Pilgrims In Their Own Land: 500 Years of Religion in America*. Marty is one of the foremost interpreters of American religion and culture.

D1316434

The Spirit of Philosophy Series

"This series of books offers the core teachings of the world's greatest philosophers, considered for the light their writings throw on the moral and material crises of our time. Repositioned in this way, philosophy and the great philosophers may once again serve humankind's eternal and ever-new need to understand who we are, why we are here, and how we are to live."

Jacob Needleman, Ph.D.
Series Editor

In the same series

Emerson by Richard Geldard
Hume by David Appelbaum
Kant by David Appelbaum
Nietzsche by Philip Novak
Wittgenstein by H. L. Finch

THE SPIRIT OF PHILOSOPHY SERIES

The Vision of James

Introduced and edited by
Stephen C. Rowe

ELEMENT
Rockport, Massachusetts ● Shaftesbury, Dorset
Brisbane, Queensland

To Diane

First published in the U.S.A. in 1996 by
Element Books, Inc.
42 Broadway, Rockport, MA 01966

Published in Great Britain in 1996 by
Element Books Limited
Shaftesbury, Dorset SP7 8BP

Published in Australia in 1996 by
Element Books Limited
for Jacaranda Wiley Limited
33 Park Road, Milton, Brisbane 4064

Cover design by Max Fairbrother

Designed and typeset by Linda Reed and Joss Nizan

Printed and bound in the U.S.A. by
R.R. Donnelley & Son.

Library of Congress Cataloging in Publication data available

British Library Cataloguing in Publication data available

ISBN 1-85230-895-8

CONTENTS

Foreword

Philosopher William James, more than any other American and more than most of the other moderns, invites readers into his world for a conversation. Stephen Rowe takes James up on the invitation, converses, and then continues the process by inviting his readers to converse.

Most philosophers tend to be formidable, forbidding, and sometimes even offering clenched minds. They have read their predecessors, drawn some conclusions, and offered these as finished products. There are no rough edges to what they package, no gaping seams where one can insert a fingernail, no places to find openings to pry further. Such philosophers may well be fulfilling their vocations; who is to say exactly how others are to philosophize? They may also get reputations for being deep or abstract, subtle or scowling; such reputations are what they have been courting all along. Not William James. He interpreted his mission in a very different way.

Life, James thought, appears to us in the form of a "rich thicket of reality," at which one could pull and wherein one could find clearings and passages. He could even praise the pathfinder as an especially helpful sort of being; he was a pathmaker. Not every thinker has to follow James's path, but we who do will be richer for the experience, as Rowe's own work here testifies.

Many have taken James up on his invitation. Titles of books about him and his work often provide evidences. Thus Jacques Barzun has written *A Stroll With William James*. A stroll. Not a climb, an assault, a charge or a dash. A stroll implies a form of walking that permits meandering; one does it for exercise, for its own sake, as it were. There may be no specific goal: one comes across marvelous surprises along the way, but they have been unsought and are welcomed almost as accidental enrichments. It is sometimes pointed out that one can engage in purposive walking, as celebrities may do when they have to hurry through a room of those who want autographs. And there is a way of standing or walking that, by the very body English, says, "come along, or come on up and let's visit."

I have chosen to be as informal and meandering as a strolling, conversing Rowe-plus-James combination lets us be. But there are more pointed and semi-technical ways of grasping what books like this about philosophers such as James are about. Many of us—I think of British philosopher Michael Oakeshott and the Canadian, Bernard Lonergan, or the American theologian David Tracy—have put energy into distinguishing between "argument" and "conversation." In the present case, we are not being invited to argue but to converse about what Rowe calls James's "vision."

Most philosophers argue, that is, they "know" an answer or at least have a strong hypothesis, and then let the answer guide what follows. They engage someone else with any of three aims in view: 1) not to be defeated in argument; 2) to defeat the other, in the eyes of bystanders and referees; 3) to convert him or her, to get him or her willingly to see the superiority of what the opponent has been offering.

Conversation is different. It is guided not by the answer but by the question. The purpose of conversation is to come to know the other; to entertain ideas that neither has explored in detail before. There is room for serendipity, for accidental discovery. "You never know where it will take you." I make a conversational bid and you respond, in ways that I cannot foresee. At the end we shall both have grown. In this process, there is room for more risk. We never hear someone say, "Boy, did I ever win that conversation!" or "He really did defeat me in that conversation." Conversations may go smoothly or roughly, well or ill: but they go, while arguments end.

The Spirit of Philosophy series is designed to promote conversation. The editors choose authors who will treat subjects that are rich in mystery, incapable of being contained by argumentative address. Pathfinding goes on. The books are supposed to push readers to the edge of the familiar, to give them courage to explore new connections.

Sometimes such endeavors can be, to use a word enemies put upon it, a little nutty. Friedrich Nietzsche had said that you must still have some chaos in your soul to give birth to a dancing star. In many cases there is so much chaos that no dancing stars but, instead, dud firecrackers result. Not so with James. He came from a family of experimenters. His father dabbled in Swedenborgian mysticism. He and some of his siblings had their requisite cases of nerves and even breakdowns. But they did stay in the bounds of mainstream culture. Harvard, William's long-term home, was not in cloudland or lotusland, after all, but Harvard and its environs and all the cultural capitals, where his novelist brother Henry James was wont to be spotted, could be stuffy, enclosed and encysted. Thinkers there, more often than not, offered clenched minds and philosophical scowls, although one could be dazzled and informed by the intellects that paraded there.

James would rather have his readers look within and find mysteries through which they could dazzle themselves. They would be informed, not in the sense that their minds were stored with piles of data, but that they were given form so that they could receive and appraise more, so that they could grow.

The way to test what I have been saying about James and James-through-Rowe is to take the texts printed here, the morsels and snippets that serve as teasers, and engage them fearlessly. One does not have to be alive to be a conversation partner. Machiavelli described how he would dress up as he entered his library of an evening. Why dress? Because he was entering good company and would there engage and be engaged by generous minds. Think of these pages as such dress-up occasions. Whether you are in clothes for the classroom or for exercise or for bedtime, figuratively you are ready to open the door and find, on the other side, a generous spirit named William James. Let the conversation begin.

Martin E. Marty

PART ONE
General Introduction

A Biographical Introduction to William James

We may be in the universe as dogs and cats are in our libraries, seeing the books and hearing the conversation, but having no inkling of the meaning of it all.

A Pluralistic Universe

William James is perhaps the most American of all European-American philosophers. James inherited European ways of thinking and living collided in his life with the American wilderness in a most creative way. The impact drove Western categories of thought, and assumptions about the relationship between thought and life, to crisis, impasse, even death—to the very sense of dilemma and nothingness that has come to characterize culture in the twentieth century.

What is distinctive about James is that he somehow had the strength not only to experience and to articulate this collision in an extremely vivid way, but also to survive it, to go beyond it, and to emerge with a new "philosophy." Yet, like the philosophy of Socrates, at the beginning of the Western tradition, and like Zen and feminism as we receive them in our post-traditional day, there is no way James's philosophy can be contained in solely conceptual terms. What he offers is more a way of living than just a way of thinking or a set of concepts.

My suggestion to the reader is that William James is a very good person to know, that knowing him can be helpful as we struggle to live a zestfully human life in turbulent times, and that the kind of knowing involved must be that of relationship rather than conceptualization. James can be a friend to us in the very best sense of that term.

The purpose of the book you are holding is to make it possible for you to enter into the kind of relationship with James through which he becomes present and known as a friend. This purpose has guided the selection of the essays included in this volume. I think the same purpose is served by sharing my own relationship with James, something I try to do in my following essay, "Revitalizing Practice: A Conversational Encounter with William James."

Before all this, though, making James available requires a little historical context and biographical detail. Just who is this character, and out of what time and place did his wonderful presence arise? And what is this philosophy-as-way-of-life that seems so well suited to human thriving in our own time, as we slip toward a new millennium?

William James was born in New York City on 11 January 1842. He was the first of five children born to Henry James, Sr., and Mary Walsh James: Henry James, Jr., (who would become the famous novelist) in the next year, followed by Garth Wilkinson, Robertson, and Alice in 1845, 1846, and 1848 respectively. The James children were born into comfortable circumstances, with sufficient financial support from the estate of their grandfather, called "William of Albany," to place them in the class of independent wealth. The William after whom our William was named was a staunch Calvinist whose work ethic drove him to success in a number of enterprises, including the Erie Canal connecting the Hudson River with the Great Lakes. Against a background of self-righteous European expansion across the American continent, the James children grew up in a foreground of their father's rebellion against the Calvinism he had inherited. Henry Sr.'s own orientation combined the influences of the French socialist Charles Fourier with those of the Swedish mystic Emanuel Swedenborg. Henry believed that God is incarnated in all of humankind; that "the fall" is not a fundamental part of the human condition, as it was for Calvin, but rather a result of individual egotism; and that human well-being lies in giving up egotistic pursuits by joining God's work of perfecting creation through liberating the natural divinity and goodness of human beings.

Henry James, Sr. sought to protect the natural innocence and freedom of his children from the corrupting force of social institutions. He took much time and effort with his children's education, as did their mother, Mary Walsh James. As a consequence, the James children attended a number of schools and studied with private tutors in Europe and the United States, traveling or moving frequently as their father's search for the ideal model continued. It should be noted that the search continued in the home as well, where such literary and theological figures as Ralph Waldo Emerson, Horace Greeley, William Cullen Bryant, and Henry David Thoreau were likely to appear as participants in the vigorous conversation of the dinner table.

William's schooling led him to become conversant in French and German, as well as with the key issues for the culturally dominant group of which he was a member. The issues were large and far-reaching in their implications, including the range and mission of the United States both on the American continent and abroad, and the function and scope of science in relating to both the natural world and the world of human interactions.[1]

By the time William was in his teens, a definite tension between art and science began to appear in his inclinations, aptitudes, and sense of vocational direction. Between 1858 and 1861 he lived periodically in Newport, Rhode Island, and studied art in earnest, including instruction from the American painter William Morris Hunt. Then in 1861 he entered Lawrence Scientific School at Harvard, and in 1864 he began studying for the M.D. degree at Harvard Medical School. Pressure to give up art in favor of science had been very strong from James's father, as well as from the general culture of the day. James wondered from the time of his momentous decision to give up art and follow the scientific path, whether he had made the right decision, even going so far as to speak some years later about a "murdered self" left behind when he gave up art study.[2]

In 1865–66 James took time off from medical school to participate in a zoological collecting expedition with Louis Agassiz in Brazil. A few months after returning from Brazil and resuming his studies at Harvard, he withdrew again, this time to study physiology and "psychophysics" in Germany. There is evidence that he interrupted his studies this second time in order also to seek a cure for mysterious pains that had developed in his back.

In 1869 he received his only graduate degree, the M.D. from Harvard. But his health remained a problem, and he experienced bouts of deep depression or "melancholia." Finally, in April 1870, James underwent a profound crisis and emerged with an understanding of his own "death and rebirth," which he sought to articulate throughout the rest of his career. The initial articulation of this experience in his journal from 30 April 1870 is brief, and arguably one of the very central expressions of culture and the humanities in the twentieth century: "My first act of free will shall be to believe in free will."[3]

James's life is fascinating, engaging—just exactly what many people have reported about the quality of his physical presence. Above and beyond his innate charm is the fact that he embodied many of the central struggles of our era, such that he can easily become someone in and with whom we see ourselves (once again, he can become a friend). So it is tempting to move into a very detailed account of his life and of the forces that swirled through the world of William James. But that is not what is needed here. Therefore I will hold to the two momentous events described above as formative in James's life and work: the decision to enter the world of science rather than that of art, and the decision to believe in free will and to act as though it were a fact. Having indicated these two formative decisions, I find it necessary to shift into a higher gear to present other details in our thumbnail sketch, merely citing in a note what I take to be the major biographical sources.[4]

But wait! One other momentous event must be described, and that is the meeting, courtship, and marriage, in 1878, with Alice Howe Gibbens. It can be said that James's greatness centers on his response to our culture's urgent need to "return to life" (as James himself put it), to actual experience, to return *from* the abstractedness of the merely mental, intellectualistic, Cartesian self that had come to dominate Western culture in the modern period. What James returns *to* is not merely the experiential flux of random events, as is so frequently the case with Western efforts relating to the need for "return." James returns to healthy dialogue between the immediacy of "pure experience" on one hand, and appropriate thought on the other, which is to say thought chosen for its consequences in placing us with the purity and intimacy of experience. The relationship with Alice was in many ways the source of James's ability to live and articulate this return. As evidence of this I cite here only one sentence from an 1877 letter from William to Alice, one that is somewhat mysterious by itself but that communicates the power and the flavor of the relationship: "Last fall and last winter what pangs of joy it sometimes gave me to let you go! to feel that in acquiescing in your unstained, unharnessed freedom I was also asserting my deepest self, and cooperating with the whole generous life of things."5 Learning to "assert deepest self" and to let go of a more superficial self (that would, among other things, seek to control others) is at the center of the Jameses' marriage and of William's legacy to us.

Now, as a way of getting into higher gear and organizing presentation of the other significant facts of James's life and work, I propose a thesis: that he inherited Western culture at the end of the traditional period primarily in the form of dilemmas or antinomies, what later in this century came to be known as "Catch 22." In this condition, breakdown and failure of cultural function manifest as the appearance of mutually opposed, equally unacceptable options, and the loss of the graceful middle ground in which things seem to have worked out for no reason that is rational. For example, in childrearing and education, child-centered permissiveness is set against "tough love" and rigid imposition of traditional discipline.

Further, I propose that James's genius consists in the penetration of dilemma (and the haze of depression or "melancholia" in which it is frequently shrouded), and the development of a new worldview—one that can be extremely helpful to us today. Finally, it is significant that penetration occurred in a most literal way, such that James progressed in his career from the physical to the spiritual: from anatomy and physiology to psychology, to philosophy and education to religious studies, and finally to psychical research.

One other overall point should be made, before turning to facts relating to this organizing thesis. Throughout his career James exhibited a remarkable concern for the public, for an audience of fellow citizens within a public conversation, sometimes to the consternation of his more professionally oriented colleagues. He published in periodicals such as *Popular Science Monthly* and *Atlantic Monthly*, and spoke to nonprofessional audiences such as public-school teachers and groups concerned with causes like "mental hygiene" and opposition to American occupation of the Philippines after the Spanish-American War. In the midst of a young culture still in the making, and in the context of enormous enthusiasm for science, James stood for the citizen rather than the professional, the generalist rather than the specialist, and for fresh thought rather than mere procedure. He was not, then, simply a psychologist or a philosopher, an educator or a student of religion, though each of these fields claims him as one of its own from time to time. He was more like an embodiment of the spiritual-humanist perspective—the perspective that holds a vision of what humans can be and become as co-creators with God in the unfinished work of creation on this planet—in a time when much of the culture was rushing away from this perspective.

After James's "resolution" of the art-science dilemma, he began his career as an Instructor of Anatomy and Physiology at Harvard College. He pursued his interest in the German "psycho-physics," taught the first course in psychology at Harvard in 1875, and in 1878 contracted to write *The Principles of Psychology* (published in 1890). In 1879 he began teaching philosophy, and later published widely, beginning with *The Will to Believe, and Other Essays in Popular Philosophy* in 1897. In the field of education, he published *Talks to Teachers* in 1899. In 1902 he published the classic work in religious studies, *The Varieties of Religious Experience*, and in 1908–1909 he delivered the Hibbert Lectures that were published as *A Pluralistic Universe*. Finally, his interest in psychical research—and his insistence on the legitimacy and importance of such research—intensified throughout his career.[6]

At each stage of his career, and we might say at each level of the culture, from the physical to the spiritual, James met with dilemma, antinomy, Catch 22. And at each stage he pushed through the impasse, into a new orientation, a new perspective, literally a new worldview. In psychology he encountered the dilemma of determinism versus free will (in our day we might say behaviorist versus humanistic forms of psychology). In philosophy the opposition was between a German idealism abstracted from real life and responsibility, and a superficial British empiricism. In religious studies James pushed beyond the dichotomy between the transmission of dogma and the settled interpretations of established elites on the one hand, and actual experience in the lives of ordinary people on the other. And throughout his work he fought the separation between thought and action, mind and body, conception and perception, the tendency in our culture for the thinkers to be out of touch and the actors to be mindless.

What emerged as James broke through these oppositions is literally a new worldview. He discovered and articulated an ecumenical perspective that both encourages our uniqueness and gives us very good reason to celebrate the company of one another. His view has several names: it is sometimes called Radical Empiricism, stressing our need to stop retreating from experience into intellectualism, to look instead into the "thick" of existence; sometimes the Jamesian perspective is referred to as Pragmatism, meaning thought and interpretation are relative to how they position us in life, not relative in the general sense of "relativism," but relative *to* the consequences of alternative ways of thinking for our relationships; James's view is also identified as Pluralism, indicating that all of our personal and cultural thoughts and interpretations are very limited in relation to the ineffable "more" of existence, so that we have something to learn from nearly everyone.

Underlying these designations, James's orientation is more an attitude of maintaining openness to what is vital or "intimate" in life, as distinct from the older sense of "philosophy" as a set of abstract propositions. James's view, then, leaves room for both variation and growth. He tells us not what to think, but rather how to think, the consequences of choosing one way of thinking or another, and he identifies some issues we must think about— chief among which is the proper relationship between thinking itself and life overall.

Returning to my basic claim that James can be helpful to us today, it seems clear that his view is quite consistent with ecological survival, with genuine affirmation of otherness, and with the maintenance and even expansion of our highest/deepest ideals as human beings. It would take a whole other essay to say, beyond what most of us would take to be self-evident, why these particulars are what we need in the way of a worldview today.[7] Perhaps, by way of concluding this brief introduction of James, as well as of indicating how he has what we need, it would be enough to make explicit a point that has been lurking throughout these pages: James immersed himself in a culture that was coming to be dominated by science, he met head on the dilemmas and contradictions that become manifest with this dominance, and he went further to reinvent the humanities— that other side of the culture having to do with the nature and nurture of our humanity—under radically new circumstances that are otherwise more suitable to machines than to people.

And friendship is at the very heart of the matter, at the heart of James's new worldview and revival of the arts and the humanities. James makes this quite explicit when he refers to his philosophy of pragmatism as essentially friendly and genial,[8] and when he connects knowing more of the truth with the capacity for friendship:

> I merely point out to you that, as a matter of fact, certain persons do exist with an enormous capacity for friendship and for taking delight in other people's lives; and that such persons know more of truth than if their hearts were not so big.[9]

Let me conclude this introduction with the recommendation that James is definitely one of those certain persons, and that friendship with him is still possible and fruitful.

James injured his heart in 1898 while engaging in a favorite recreation—mountain climbing in the

Adirondacks. He never really recovered, and died of heart failure in 1910. Toward the end of his life he experienced deep regret over his sense that he had not completed his work, at least not in the form of a systematic philosophy, which had been the standard of success up to his time. The moral of his story might be that we are not the best judges of ourselves and our worth. The moral might also be that we await relationship with others for our own completion to occur. Following this moral, perhaps there is even a sense in which our friendship with James might be reciprocal: perhaps there is some way in which his psychic and spiritual well-being is aided by our appreciating in him what he was not able to appreciate in himself.

---

1 For background on American culture in the time of William James, see Martin E. Marty, *Modern American Religion*, vol. 1: *The Irony of It All, 1893–1919,* Chicago: University of Chicago Press, 1986, especially 64–8.

2 Cited from a James lecture in Howard M. Feinstein, *Becoming William James*, Ithaca, N.Y.: Cornell University Press, 1984, 144.

3 William James, "Diary, April 30, 1870," in John J. McDermott, ed., *William James: A Comprehensive Edition*, New York: Random House, 1967, 7–8.

4 I suggest the following biographical sources: Ralph Barton Perry, *The Thought and Character of William James*, New York: Braziller, 1954; Gay Wilson Allen, *William James: A Biography*, New York: Viking Press, 1967; R.W.B. Lewis, *The Jameses: A Family Narrative*, New York: Doubleday, 1991; Gerald E. Myers, *William James: His Life and Thought*, New Haven: Yale University Press, 1986; Howard M. Feinstein, *Becoming William James*.

5 Cited in R.W.B. Lewis, 278.

6 See Gardner Murphy and Robert O. Ballou, eds., *William James on Psychical Research*, New York: Viking Press, 1960.

7 I seek to address these particulars of a new worldview in my *Rediscovering the West: An Inquiry into Nothingness and Relatedness*, Albany, N.Y.: SUNY Press, 1994.

8 "What Pragmatism Means," in *Pragmatism*, Cambridge: Harvard University Press, 1975, 44.

9 "What Makes a Life Significant?," in *Talks to Teachers on Psychology and to Students on Some of Life's Ideals*, Cambridge: Harvard University Press, 1983, 151. Ralph Barton Perry takes this statement as the conclusion to his biography of James.

Revitalizing Practice: A Conversational Encounter with William James

The temperature was perfect either inside or outside the cabin, the moon rose and hung above the scene before midnight, leaving only a few of the larger stars visible, and I got into a state of spiritual alertness of the most vital description. . . . The intense significance of some sort, of the whole scene, if one could only *tell* the significance; the intense inhuman remoteness of its inner life, and yet the intense *appeal* of it; its everlasting freshness and its immemorial antiquity and decay; its utter Americanism, and every sort of patriotic suggestiveness, and you, and my relation to you part and parcel of it all. . . . In point of fact, I can't find a single word for all that significance, and don't know what it was significant of, so there it remains, a mere boulder of *impression*. Doubtless in more ways than one, though, things in the Edinburgh lectures will be traceable to it.

—William James, 1898, letter to his wife

One time James said that "Any author is easy if you can catch the centre of his vision."[1] Out of my own encounter with James I have come to see that, underneath the many modes and occasions of his work, the center of his vision is conversation. His pluralistic worldview and his engaging temperament are expressed in an attitude that is larger than mere tolerance: "Hands off: neither the whole of truth, nor the whole of good, is revealed to any single observer, although each observer gains a partial superiority of insight from the peculiar position in which he stands."[2] James is *interested* in those partial superiorities and peculiar positions, interested in learning more and continuing to grow, interested in conversation as the kind of relational encounter in which learning and growth occur. He is interested, then, not just because he wants to know more, but because of what the practice of conversation does for us, for the energy that becomes available through conversational encounter.

In the same way that we cannot read the dialogues of Socrates without understanding dialogue as a transformative practice and without *becoming* dialogical, so we cannot read James without understanding conversation. In fact, conversation in James is very similar to dialogue in Socrates: it is a kind of relationship that has transformative effects, a kind through which the mature or fully formed human being emerges. Conversation is an activity much deeper and more significant than either the simple transmission of concepts or the expression of personal feeling; reading James with the assumption that he is working in either of these more familiar genres will cause him to be missed and violated.[3]

I have come to see that the conversation between James and people in our time is about revitalization, about overcoming the numbness, negativity, and self-destructive cynicism that infect people in the midst of post-traditional cultural confusion. The thesis of this introductory essay is that conversing with James through reading him can be a transformative, revitalizing practice, that the conversation with him can be helpful in our real life problems.

The writings of James included in this volume are ordered as if he were conversing with us today;[4] the table of contents of this volume reflects the conversational encounter of the essay you are reading now. My introduction of James, then, becomes an instance of the conversational practice it seeks to celebrate in James and to invoke in the reader. To make more vivid the strands of conversation between this introduction and the essays that follow, I have placed at the beginning of each essay the statement from it that appears in this introduction.

I turn now to my conversation with James.

"One Step Further": Positing Life

What if life is so structured that all problems arise because of our human rejection of the gift quality of life, and our resulting inability to locate our own vitality and genuine selfhood? Suppose that this rejection is really an obstruction, and that what stands between us and our well-being is a deep fear of trusting what is beyond our control, mixed—in ever more curious ways in the various individuals of the world—with a primal arrogance that we can control what is beyond our fear. The root human problem, then, would be that we identify with combinations of this fear and arrogance, mistakenly identifying as *ourselves* that which actually alienates us from ourselves.

The salvation from this condition can be stated only as a paradox or riddle, a circumstance of the co-presence of two realities that appear to be in opposition but are not. On one side we must renounce entirely our efforts at control, accepting the "death" of all our schemes and techniques, even the death of ourselves in the ego sense. The other side of the Jamesian paradox is that we must even go so far as to reject the temptation to think that this renunciation requires that we do nothing or that we discount the importance of human action. Complete renunciation, paradoxically, requires that we completely accept what is, including the actualities of the human condition—one of which is the necessity of choice and action. Complete renunciation thus becomes a return, a willingness to thrive, a celebration of the gift of life as it is given to us, as, in the words of Hannah Arendt, "a free gift from nowhere."[5]

Here, I suggest, is the vision of William James in miniature, his discovery of what it means to be loyal "to our common mother."[6] He said it very directly in one of his popular essays, "The Gospel of Relaxation":

> The way to do it [that is, anything], paradoxical as it may seem, is genuinely not to care whether you are doing it or not. Then, possibly, by the grace of God, you may all at once find that you *are* doing it, and having learned what the trick feels like, you may (again by the grace of God) be enabled to go on.[7]

Of course, we need to note the paradoxical quality of this situation in which James has made the choice to "do it" and to "go on"—not at all to "not care" altogether!

The secret is to "not care" or to "*Unclamp*, in a word, your intellectual and practical machinery, and let it run free. . . ."[8] This allows us to "descend to a more profound and primitive level," and to experience "The intense interest that life can assume when brought down to the non-thinking level, the level of pure sensorial perception. . . ."9 In another statement of this root paradox James speaks of our need to renounce efforts at "being good": "Sincerely to give up one's conceit or hope of being good in one's own right is the only door to the universe's deeper reaches."10

But, again, the paradox is that this renunciation is *not*, for James, a simple letting go or "go with the flow" approach. It is not the opposite of action; in fact, the renunciation James champions actually vitalizes choice and responsibility rather than diminishing them, elevating action above the mere laborings of the ego. James states this in terms of "the return to life":

> The return to life can't come about by talking. It is an *act*; to make you return to life, I must set an example for your imitation, I must deafen you to talk, or to the importance of talk, by showing you, as Bergson does, that the concepts we talk with are made for purposes of *practice* and not for purposes of insight.11

The character and depth of James's emphasis on action, on return as an act, is perhaps most fully revealed in his personal life. James, in his struggles with "melancholia," came to the question of suicide, even to the sense of suicide as the most authentic expression of free will: "Hitherto, when I have felt like taking a free initiative, like daring to act originally, without carefully waiting for contemplation of the external world to determine all for me, suicide seemed like the most manly form to put my daring into. . . ."12 The crucial point in his life, the "return," came in 1870 when he decided to go one step further: ". . . now I will go a step further with my will, not only act with it, but believe as well; believe in my individual reality and creative power. . . . I will posit life."[13] Everything depends on this "step further."

James's radical positing of life, then, is based on an experience of vitality (or "grace") that lies beyond the usual understanding of both "not caring" or renunciation on one hand, and "doing it" or action on the other. He went beyond both the deep fear of trusting and the primal arrogance of control, beyond the oppositions of life that drive one to impossibility or unacceptable alternatives; for "not caring" without action leads to fear, and action without the "not caring" becomes arrogance. In fact, for James, the "facts" of a certain experience of death, or despair of the ordinary alternatives, seem unavoidable in the process of coming to one's full vitality.

> Briefly, the facts I have in mind may all be described as experiences of an unexpected life succeeding upon death. By this I don't mean immortality, or the death of the body. I mean the deathlike termination of certain mental processes within the individual's experience, processes that run to failure, and in some individuals, at least, eventuate in despair. . . .
>
> The phenomenon is that of new ranges of life succeeding on our most despairing moments. There are resources in us that naturalism with its literal and legal virtues never recks of, possibilities that take our breath away, of another kind of happiness and power, based on giving up our own will and letting something higher work for us, and these seem to show a world wider than either physics or philistine ethics can imagine.[14]

The movement to genuine human action and to this "wider world" is possible, as James says, due to "the grace of God." And yet there is something we can do about it, a way to nurture this experience, encourage the co-presence, learn to live the paradox of revitalization. Learning to live the paradox is at the center of our conversation with James.

Choice, Intimacy, and Pragmatism

The first thing we must do is to come to a proper understanding of the role of philosophy in relation to vitality, revitalization, and "return to life." To put it more baldly, the question is: just what are we doing here, with you reading, me writing, and both of us together somehow pursuing the vitality of another? What is this practice of philosophy in which we are engaged, and what might we expect from it in terms of real results for living and not just for conceptualizing? Part of what is so helpful about James is that, given his pragmatic orientation, he has real and compelling answers to these questions.

For James, there are two aspects to philosophy. The first is common to all people, and arises from the fact that all people conceive of the world based on the analogy of one of its parts: ". . . after the analogy of some particular feature of it which has particularly captivated their attention."[15] Difficulties and disagreements result from the fact that everyone is "prone to claim that his conclusions are the only logical ones, that they are necessities of universal reason, they being all the while, at bottom, accidents more or less of personal vision. . . ."[16]

In understanding James it is important to appreciate the original or basic context out of which the analogies appear in the early stage of both individual development and the history of culture:

> The eeriness of the world, the mischief and the manyness, the littleness of the forces, the magical surprises, the unaccountability of every agent, these surely are the characters most impressive at that stage of culture. . . . Nature, more demonic than divine, is above all things *multifarious.* So many creatures that feed or threaten, that help or crush, so many beings to hate or love, to understand or start at. . . . The symbol of nature at this stage, as Paulsen well says, is the sphinx, under whose nourishing breasts the tearing claws are visible.[17]

Out of this original experience of the world, some one feature will so impress us that we henceforth relate to the whole of life on the analogy of that particular feature. In its first aspect, then, "philosophy is the expression of a man's intimate character. . . ."[18]

The second aspect of philosophy arises out of the human ability to become conscious of what it was from "the mischief and the manyness" that impressed us and became our "analogy," and then to envision and evaluate alternative orientations in life, and to *make choices* that actually *change* our analogy. Philosophy in the second aspect is thus "the deliberately adopted reactions of human characters. . . ."[19]

While the first aspect of philosophy is shared by all people, the second is not (which is by no means to say it is the preserve of professional philosophers, who frequently become lost in the "abuse of technicality"[20]). What distinguishes the second aspect is reason, in the sense of our human ability to become conscious of what analogy has been impressed upon us and to choose to have it be otherwise—to choose a different analogy or life orientation: "Common men find themselves inheriting their beliefs, they know not how. They jump into them with both feet, and stand there. Philosophers must do more; they must first get reason's licence for them. . . ."[21] The significance in James of this human ability to become conscious and to choose cannot be overemphasized. He goes so far as to see this ability in terms of the working of the universe: "Philosophies are intimate parts of the universe, they express something of its own thought of itself. A philosophy may indeed be a most momentous reaction of the universe upon itself."[22] But, again, we must be careful not to look automatically to professional philosophers for a role model in this; they, much more than others it seems, too frequently make themselves absurd by their failure to acknowledge their choice of a philosophy, by their insistence that their philosophy represents just "the way things are."

James's recommendation as to the criteria for our choice of philosophy or life orientation centers not on the universe in general but rather on the Earth as our "common mother." He speaks of a "deep agreement" and "one deep concern":

> . . . all the parties are human beings with the same essential interests, and no one of them is the wholly perverse demon which another often imagines him to be. Both are loyal to the world that bears them; neither wishes to spoil it; neither wishes to regard it as an insane incoherence; both want to keep it as a universe of some kind; and their differences are all secondary to this deep agreement. . . . [A]ll such differences are minor matters which ought to be subordinated in view of the fact that, whether we be empiricists or rationalists, we are, ourselves, parts of the universe and share the same one deep concern

in its destinies. We crave alike to feel more truly at
home with it, and to contribute our mite to its ame-
lioration.[23]

In relation to this profound commonness James proclaims that he is "as good a son as any rationalist among
you to our common mother."[24] It is on this same ground
that he goes on to recommend that we make our choices
of philosophy under the criterion of intimacy: Does a
philosophy that we might choose place us more intimately in the world, or does it make us foreigners? Does it
have a sympathetic or a cynical temper? Is it more spiritualistic or more materialistic? Does it incline more toward
breasts or claws? According to James, the choice is ours,
and the choice of intimacy is what puts us in touch with
vitality, with "new ranges of life," "possibilities that take
our breath away, of another kind of happiness and
power."

This fundamental choice of philosophy or life orientation is utterly momentous. It is momentous for us individually and for those around us, in something like the
American attitude of positive thinking that James both
generates and reflects—something like self-fulfilling
prophecy. For James it is possible to identify human
problems and to act so as to change our circumstance in
ways that are fundamental, as he did in his own life,
overcoming depression and "positing life." This Jamesian
attitude toward the possibility of momentous choice
applies not only to individual life but also to public poli-
cy. Here he states it in terms of the possibility of the
human race's finding a "moral equivalent of war".

> . . . inordinate ambitions are the soul of every patrio-
> tism, and the possibility of violent death the soul of

all romance. The militarily patriotic and romantic-minded everywhere, and especially the professional military class, refuse to admit for a moment that war may be a transitory phenomenon in social evolution.

. . . So long as anti-militarists propose no substitute for war's disciplinary function, no *moral equivalent* of war, analogous, as one might say, to the mechanical equivalent of heat, so long they fail to realize the full inwardness of the situation.[25]

But the grandeur of being human, for James, goes even further than psychological and social construction. It includes our ability to support the very presence of certain transhuman realities—like love or beauty, or even God—that might not otherwise be able to be present in the world. In other words, there are certain realities whose very existence (at least on Earth) depend, in part, on the human willingness to believe in them. In his well-known essay "The Will to Believe," James states this radical view of the priority of will over belief (one we have seen before in relation to his personal crisis), setting it over against "snarling logicality:"

. . . one who should shut himself up in snarling logicality and try to make the gods extort his recognition willy-nilly, or not get it at all, might cut himself off forever from his only opportunity of making the gods' acquaintance. This feeling, forced on us we know not whence, that by obstinately believing that there are gods (although not to do so would be so easy both for our logic and our life) we are doing the universe the deepest service we can, seems part of the living essence of the religious hypothesis.[26]

So, returning to the concern with which we began this section, we can say that the practice of philosophy—this reading, writing, all this making of distinctions and references near and far—is for the sake of our *choice*, our decision and our will. Our "philosophy" is literally the articulation of our decision to "posit life"—or not. Articulation helps in the choosing since it makes the options more visible and hence more conscious, thereby expanding the scope of choice. And the choice is momentous not only for us and our immediate community, but also in the largest sense of the working of reality itself. It is not going too far to say that for James human choice is a way of joining God directly in the ongoing work of creation, "doing the universe the deepest service we can." In any intimate view, our choice matters very much.

James's own particular choice of philosophy is hard to pin down. It is whatever helps move in the direction of greater intimacy and access to the "deeper riches" of genuine vitality. James's view is "pragmatism," which appears to be indeterminate or vague, loose or even subjectivist if it is measured against traditional standards of intellectual formula and fixed position. Yet James makes it clear that he has no apology for his "genial" view (to which he refers in female terms, perhaps parallel to his references to the Earth as our "common mother"):

> You see by this what I meant when I called pragmatism a mediator and reconciler and said, borrowing the word from Papini, that she "unstiffens" our theories. She has in fact no prejudices whatever, no obstructive dogmas, no rigid canons of what shall count as proof. She is completely genial. She will entertain any hypothesis, she will consider any

evidence. It follows that in the religious field she is at great advantage both over positivistic empiricism, with its anti-theological bias, and over religious rationalism, with its exclusive interest in the remote, the noble, the simple, and the abstract in the way of conception. . . .

. . . Her manners are as various and flexible, her resources as rich and endless, and her conclusions as friendly as those of mother nature.[27]

But James is no relativist! There certainly are views that are not friendly, such as the empiricism and the rationalism he mentions above, so that his own Zen-like orientation must not be mistaken for mere relaxation.

To move closer to James's way of return, or positing life, we now turn to two quite characteristic approaches that are not effective, that cause people to displace or misidentify their vitality, placing themselves in positions of foreignness. Then we shall come back more directly to the friendliness that James recommends.

Actionlessness, Intellectualism, and Pluralism

James, as we have seen, sometimes identifies rationalism and empiricism as the prevailing positions opposing the pragmatic pluralism he recommends. The problem with rationalism (defined as understanding parts by their larger wholes) is that it is abstracted and so heavily conceptual, remote from the pulsing experience of real life. On the other hand, empiricism (understanding wholes by their parts) tends to be shallow, tied up in both intellectual "snarling logicality" and a materialism that recognizes only *things*, to the exclusion of the experience of relation or connectedness. If the vision of rationalism is *up*, and that of empiricism is *lateral*, then the pragmatic alternative of James is *downward*, into the *thick* of existence, "flat on its belly in the middle of experience, in the very thick of its sand and gravel. . . ."[28]

The abstracted upwardness of rationalism and the frustrating superficiality of empiricism certainly do indicate, for James, significant ways of failing to make contact with vitality. To these ways he juxtaposes "radical empiricism" as a synonym for the Jamesian alternative, one that recognizes both the depth or thickness of experience and the experience of relation.

However, I think there is in James a deeper indication of the typical ways that people make bad choices in their philosophy. These ways correspond with the basic problems of fear and arrogance: "not caring" without action on one hand, and "doing it" without "unclamping" on the other—the two ways discussed at the beginning of this essay that need to be paradoxically copresent, the two ways that result from failure of copresence. The two failed ways become visible in James's mature work as "all-form" actionlessness and the rigid control of "vicious intellectualism." A little background and context will help at this point.

In 1909, the year before his death, James delivered the prestigious Hibbert Lectures at Oxford University. In these lectures, later published under the title of *A Pluralistic Universe*, James quite explicitly pursues "intimacy," or the kind of philosophical orientation that places us most directly in relation to vitality. As his pursuit progresses, he first dismisses materialism as a position of foreignness. He then moves on to the traditional dualistic theism, the "official" position of much of the culture, which is also found to be quite foreign: in "orthodox theism," "God is not heart of our heart and reason of our reason, but our magistrate, rather; and mechanically to obey his commands, however strange they may be, remains our only moral duty."[29]

Having decided to ignore "old-fashioned dualistic theism," James next turns to the more spiritual view, which he also identifies as pantheistic: "the vision of God as the indwelling divine rather than the external creator, and of human life as part and parcel of that deep reality."[30] He then immediately breaks this more intimate species of philosophical orientation into two subspecies, one monistic and the other pluralistic. "For monism, the world is no collection, but one great all-inclusive fact outside of which is nothing—nothing is its only alternative."[31] Pluralism, on the other hand, is "more like a federal republic than like an empire or a kingdom. However much may be collected, however much may report itself as present at any effective center of consciousness or action, something else is self-governed and absent and unreduced to unity."[32] In other words, in monism (or the "all-form" philosophy) there are finally no distinctions between anything and anything else and everything, whereas in pluralism (or the "each-form" view) separate entities, including both humans and God, actually exist in themselves and act.

At the beginning of *A Pluralistic Universe* James says that his main purpose in the lectures to follow will be to offer a sort of dialogue between the popular monistic view and his pluralistic alternative, arguing that the pluralistic is the option of greater intimacy. It is in the context of this dialogue and argument that the problems of actionlessness and "vicious intellectualism" arise. Since the underlying structure and purpose of *A Pluralistic Universe* is movement from the outside in, from the less to the more intimate life orientation, we can say that these two problems are our two deepest obstacles to intimacy or vitality.

In monism actionlessness is a problem in that if everything is the "all-form" or God, and if no distinctions are really possible, then it is impossible for either humans *or God* to actually ever *do* anything. Everything is just as it is; everything happens just as it must; there is nothing to do, except, perhaps, to stop trying to do anything. All we can do is to "unclamp," "not care," relax.

There is, of course, a *partial* truth to this orientation, a moment in experience when it is even fully true, or when it serves as an important corrective to certain human illusions about our ability to control life. But taken by itself and generalized to an orientation to life as a whole, this view is unworkable—and dangerous. Its pragmatic consequences are inaction, absence of discipline or strenuousness, failure of compassion, default to whatever values prevail by whatever means—"moral holiday" in James's terms.[33]

The pragmatic consequence of fearfulness enters into this view in that not only does human helplessness follow, the sense that there is nothing we can do to protect ourselves or lessen our chances of demise, but so also does divine inaction follow. God, as James points out again and again, can do nothing in this philosophy. Hence no appeal is possible, and no inkling of God's plan or purpose is possible, and neither is any sense of mercy or personal relationship. God, somewhat like Aristotle's "Unmoved Mover," *just is*, and, moreover, is thoroughly indistinguishable from *what is*. There is, then, no accounting for the realities of evil, suffering, death, and other "tremendous irrationalities"[34] in the universe, and no guarantee whatsoever that these do not constitute the "bottom line" in our own existence. How could this view not lead to the sort of chronic fearfulness or wariness, generalized insecurity or even paranoia, that would block us from our own vitality?

The second problem associated with monism is "vicious intellectualism": *"The treating of a name as excluding from the fact named what the name's definition fails positively to include, is what I call 'vicious intellectualism.'* . . . [A] person whom you have once called an 'equestrian' is thereby forever made unable to walk on his own feet."[35] "Vicious intellectualism" is a retreat from the complexities of real life into intellectual formulations that have become sealed off from any new insight or energy from lived experience. As James has made clear in his definition of philosophy as a way of human choice to move from a more foreign to a more intimate way of living, the intellect is very important in human life. As an essential organ of consciousness, it makes possible choice and action. But it serves its proper function only in the ongoing pragmatic relationship with "pure experience" and real life as a whole. When it ascends to a position of dominance over experience, the intellect becomes vicious in its refusal to listen to experience, insisting that the relationship run one way only, from intellectual conclusions to experience. It violates real life.

According to James, "vicious intellectualism" is a pervasive problem in Western culture, which, correctly or incorrectly, he traces to Socrates and Plato:

> Intellectualism in the vicious sense began when Socrates and Plato taught that what a thing really is, is told us by its definition. Ever since Socrates we have been taught that reality consists of essences,

not of appearances, and that the essences of things
are known whenever we know their definitions.[36]

We are talking here about the stance that philosophers
have taken in Western culture, but also, and more importantly, about a general disposition and temptation among
Western people. We are talking about a retreat from real
life, into a realm that is essentially mental (not physical,
emotional, spiritual, etc.) in which conclusions are fash-
ioned, and a subsequent posture in lived life that insists
that all relationships confirm the foregone conclusions.

Monism in particular, for James, embodies this disposition in heightened form—its degree of failure and
dangerousness corresponding to its relatively high
degree of closeness to intimacy. It seems evident that
monism's failure arises from valuing the order of the
intellect more than monism's own deepest intuition of
oneness and rightness in the universe. And the underlying flaw of human arrogance is likewise revealed in
monism's internal conflict between the spiritual wish to
accept life on the one hand, and the egotistical desire to
contain and control through intellectual formulation on
the other.

To select a metaphor James might like: with "vicious
intellectualism," access to vitality is impossible because
we have retreated from the storm of real life, sealing ourselves off in the small cabin of the intellect, devoting ourselves to ever more insulation and chinking. Some form
of insanity, fanaticism, viciousness, or suffocation seems
inevitable. As many of us well know, cabin fever is no
joke; it can turn even the most gentle intuition of oneness into a raving, chaotic manyness.

Returning to monism as the philosophical orientation that stands closest to pluralism, the most intimate

orientation in life, we can understand the problems associated with monism to be our deepest or most basic problems in life. The problems of actionlessness and the resulting fear on one side, and arrogant intellectualism on the other, are our deepest obstacles to intimacy and full vitality. Actionlessness and intellectualism are like the cherubim and the flaming sword that God placed at the gate to the Garden of Eden after Adam and Eve were ejected, signifying no admission in the future, and representing the dangers that appear when we come close. And yet, for James, admission is possible. He means to suggest something this radical by presenting pluralism as the orientation that lies between and beyond the opposed relation of "not caring" and "doing it."

Relationship, Will, and Radical Empiricism

Taking seriously the structure of James' late work, its movement from the most foreign to the most intimate orientations in life, we now come to the question: In positive terms, *what is* pluralism, radical empiricism, or pragmatism as a philosophy of intimacy, return, friendliness, and access to vitality?

To find an answer to this question that is worth having, one that is anything other than a bag of concepts contributing to the "conceptual decomposition of life"[37] that James so abhorred, we must examine our approach, the very presuppositions of our own seeking and finding. This examination and change of stance from the conceptual to one that is appropriate to our life in a more holistic sense, is an essential part of answering the question of how revitalization or "return to life" is possible. This is so because revitalization, for James, is much more than a better way of thinking, though a better way of thinking can certainly help; the point is that thinking can help with something much larger than thinking as an end in itself.

James can guide us in this examination of our own approach if we pay attention to his way of articulating the most intimate and vital life orientation. Over the years, his way of articulation has been the source of debate; there has been much comment on the unsystematic quality of his work, on the fact that he skips around, winds back, repeats, sometimes meanders. Some have suggested that this quality of his communication is a function of his erratic character, or of the genius of his work, which is just barely under his control. Others have regretted his style, lamenting, along with James himself at some moments toward the end of his life, that he never did a "systematic" work.

My own understanding is that James's work is profoundly and unavoidably *relational*, not just in the intellectual "position" he takes, but in the very form or genre of his writing. He always speaks to people, with people, from the inside of a conversation, never the outside. The conversation within which he speaks is broad, including persons from Eastern cultures, and it is deep, including even himself as well as God and other possible psychical entities. But he never strays from the nexus of vital relationship. He never allows his own self to slip out of relationship, to lose itself in his own subjectivity (though he certainly knew this problem through his bouts with "melancholia"). And he never abstracts to make an object of the other with whom he is in conversation, which is to say he remains open to the possibility of further insight from the irreducible other. Here, I suggest, is the genius of James and the cause of the extreme frustration of his work to both the psychological reader seeking identity with James in his private struggles and the strictly intellectual observer looking only for concepts: James speaks from relationship and he is unrelenting in his insistence on relationship with his reader—refusing displacement into either the subjective or the objective.

So the first and most general point that James makes about "return" is that access to our vitality can occur only through relationship, not through drawing back into either "morbid introspection"[38] or lofty conceptualization. And relationship is inevitably concrete, specific, contingent, and beyond our control; any genuine relationship is *radically* empirical. In response to these difficult realities, there are powerful parts of ourselves that do not wish to hear that "relationship" contains the answer to our problems. (Our culture teaches us to be either psychologists or intellectuals, beings both of whom are unwilling or unable to stay with the vitalizing relational quality of existence.) We read James with confusion or vexation until we accept this most basic point.

Let us, then, revise our approach, resolving to be faithful to relationship with James, and taking a moment to be clear about where we stand in the relationship. My own stand, as the reader by now knows, is that we are urgently in need of revitalization: "The beginning point is our actual situation: an unsteadiness in our relations with each other, a certain dullness within ourselves, and an underlying absence of vision or deep orientation, as though we have forgotten how to live a human life. We need revitalization before we forget that revitalization is what we need."[39] This, as I have said earlier, is the thesis informing my own presence in the conversation of this essay and in the selection from James's work. My point to the reader now, though, is not only to be aware of

James and of the perspective of your interpreter, but, just
as importantly, to be aware of *your own* presence in the
conversation.

My first suggestion as to what James is saying about
our revitalization, then, is that it occurs—strange and
even dangerous as this might seem at first—through relationship rather than through either introspection or conceptualization. The alternative approaches to achieving
vitality correspond to the fearful "not caring" and the
arrogant "doing it" discussed earlier. Relationship is distinct from these alternatives, and beyond their either/or
opposition. Consistent with the "friendliness" of pragmatism, relationship is "a mediator and reconciler."

The second suggestion is that revitalization must
occur at the level of *will*. This is to say that James speaks
both from and to a sense of self much deeper than the
understandings that had come to be taken for granted in
Western culture. In our time, for example, and in the
context of East–West dialogue, John B. Cobb, Jr. says that
the West lacks "a depth of insight into the nature of reality."[40] James is a Western visionary who saw and
responded to this problem, specifically in understandings
of self. It is no wonder that Easterners refer to James as
an exception to the prevailing Western orientation, an
exception quite compatible with Eastern insight.[41]

Will, in James, like "genuine Self" in Zen, is hard to
pin down (perhaps in the same way that it is hard to
understand the presence of Christ in or through the self
in Christianity: "it is no longer I who live, but Christ who
lives in me," Galatians 2:20). Will is underneath both the
feelings of subjectivity and the conceptual formulations of
objectivity. It is behind or, in the term of Kitaro Nishida,
"transdescends"[42] any effort to grasp self. Our will or
deep self cannot be discovered and strengthened through

subjective introspection or through objective construction, but only through relationship. In the conversational relationship with our era of post-objectivism or post-foundationalism, James especially reminds us of the need to maintain certain of our more humane "instinctive reactions," as against the danger of subjectivism:

> There are *some* instinctive reactions which I, for one, will not tamper with. The only remaining alternative [to objectivism, which inevitably becomes determinism], the attitude of gnostical romanticism, wrenches my personal instincts in quite as violent a way. It falsifies the simple objectivity of their deliverance. It makes the goose-flesh the murder excites in me a sufficient reason for the perpetration of the crime. It transforms life from a tragic reality into an insincere melodramatic exhibition, as foul or as tawdry as anyone's diseased curiosity pleases to carry it out. . . . it leaves me in presence of a sort of subjective carrion considerably more noisome than the objective carrion I called it in to take away.[43]

In our relationship with James in this essay thus far, we have encountered will in the personal crisis of 1870, where will made it possible for him to go beyond his melancholia, to both believe and act in such a way as to "posit life." Will has also surfaced in terms of that human capacity by which we are able to become aware of the feature of early experience that became our analogy for life as a whole, and to choose a more intimate philosophy or life orientation. And we have seen will and its significance in James's suggestion that there are transhuman realities whose very ability to be present on Earth may depend in part on the human willingness to sustain a belief in them and to *act* as if they existed.

Will indicates a way of relating to the self beyond any sense in which it can be objectified or conceptualized, a way of caring for the self, and thus also a way of curing the self of its egotistical preoccupations and fears. This way of relating to the self is beyond psychology, at least in the usual sense of that term. In fact, James's way of going beyond psychology is precisely the way that some of the more astute commentators on our psychological century have said we need. One of them, Ira Progoff says: "Although it began as part of the protest against religion, the net result of modern psychology has been to reaffirm man's experience of himself as a spiritual being" and the need for "a soul beyond psychology."[44] It should be noted as well that James's going beyond has indeed (and with some irony, since James is a parent of American psychology) been the inspiration of many groups and persons in this century, for example, Alcoholics Anonymous.

The going beyond any objectification of self is radical, making choice and real change of the self possible. It is radical in the sense that will—and contact with our deepest source of vitality—arises out of "pure experience" and the descent to a "more profound and primitive level" of "pure sensorial experience." Though it is not exactly clear, to me at least, from James's work, he seems to be recommending some form of meditation or "relaxation" as a way of strengthening the will and hence revitalizing.[45] It is clear, though, that self at the level of will, underneath both "not caring" and "doing it," cannot be grasped by ordinary consciousness, so that efforts at description are like "trying to turn up the gas quickly enough to see how the darkness looks."[46]

For James, a healthy relationship to the self is more like one of educator to student than of psychologist to patient; it is more like art than science:

> . . . sciences never generate arts directly out of them-
> selves. An intermediary inventive mind must make
> the application, by using its originality. . . .
>
> . . . A science only lays down lines within
> which the rules of the art must fall, laws which the
> follower of the art must not transgress; but what par-
> ticular thing he shall positively do within those lines
> is left exclusively to his own genius. One genius will
> do his work well and succeed in one way, whilst
> another succeeds as well quite differently; yet nei-
> ther will transgress the lines. . . .
>
> To know psychology, therefore, is absolutely no
> guarantee that we shall be good teachers. To
> advance to that result we must have an additional
> endowment altogether, a happy tact and ingenuity
> to tell us what definite things to say and do when
> the pupil is before us. That ingenuity in meeting and
> pursuing the pupil, that tact for the concrete situa-
> tion, though they are the alpha and omega of the
> teacher's art, are things to which psychology cannot
> help us in the least.[47]

Our will is what makes it possible for us to exercise the
additional endowment of tact and ingenuity necessary to
vital living.

Conversation, Vitality, and the Lesson

My third suggestion of what James is saying about our
revitalization brings us back to the structure of *A
Pluralistic Universe* and our relationship with him
through this particular text. The strategy for that text is
relationship with the reader that moves from the foreign

to the intimate philosophy or life orientation. My thesis is that when James gets to the most intimate orientation—"pluralism," "radical empiricism," or "pragmatism"—he is, in effect, acting as a philosophical educator, working in the medium of educational conversation and exercising the "tact and ingenuity" that can strengthen the will and place it in vital relationship.

Several other points in *A Pluralistic Universe*, beyond those already mentioned, serve as strengthening and locating functions in relation to our will or deep self. Lifting these points out of the James texts—abstracting them from the conversation into which they are woven—is perhaps permissible in order to move them into the conversation of this essay, especially since this essay is an invitation to the original James texts. By way of concluding and of encouraging the reader to continue in the conversation with James, I mention these few other points.

In *A Pluralistic Universe* James presents his radical reading of the Western tradition: "The ruling tradition in philosophy has always been the Platonistic and Aristotelian belief that fixity is a nobler and worthier thing than change."[48] The immediate consequence of this belief has been the preference for concepts over experience: "Concepts, being themselves fixities, agree best with this fixed nature of truth, so that for any knowledge of ours to be quite true it must be knowledge by universal concepts rather than by particular experiences, for these notoriously are mutable and corruptible."[49] This awareness of the dominant tradition, the tradition of rationalism, whose extreme expression is intellectualism, led James to conclude that "philosophy had been on a false scent ever since the days of Socrates and Plato. . . ."[50]

The remedy for rationalism's tyranny of concepts over experience is twofold. First, it is necessary to realize that concepts and experience are both required and complementary:

> Direct acquaintance and conceptual knowledge are thus complementary of each other; each remedies the other's defects. If what we care most about be the synoptic treatment of phenomena, the vision of the far and the gathering of the scattered like, we must follow the conceptual method. But if, as metaphysicians, we are more curious about the inner nature of reality or about what really makes it go, we must turn our backs upon our winged concepts altogether, and bury ourselves in the thickness of those passing moments over the surface of which they fly, and on particular points of which they occasionally rest and perch.[51]

This broadly comparative and historical awareness, of which James is a pioneer in the post-traditional period that begins with the end of his century and the beginning of ours, gives rise to the second element of remedy. It is an inversion of the traditional relationship between the conceptual and the experiential functions of human life as it had been construed in the West. James does this partially as a corrective to the historic imbalance and partially because of the real priority of experience over thought: "The essence of life is its continuously changing character; but our concepts are all discontinuous and fixed, . . . not *parts* of reality, not real positions taken by it, but *suppositions* rather, notes taken by ourselves, and you can no more dip up the substance of reality with them than you can dip up water with a net, however finely meshed."[52]

The second element of remedy for rationalism, then, is to learn to "think in nonconceptualized terms."[53] This involves a change in life orientation so fundamental that it is an "inner catastrophe" or death and rebirth experience, followed by a "return to life." This change is beyond the reach of words:

> I went thus through the 'inner catastrophe' of which I spoke in the last lecture; I had literally come to the end of my conceptual stock-in-trade, I was bankrupt intellectually, and had to change my base. No words of mine will probably convert you, for words can be the names only of concepts. But if any of you try sincerely and pertinaciously on your own separate accounts to intellectualize reality, you may be similarly driven to a change of front. I say no more: I must leave life to teach the lesson.[54]

The *consequence* of this fundamental lesson is precisely *vitality* or the revitalization that comes through access to a "wider self," "central self," or "higher consciousness":

> Every bit of us at every moment is part and parcel of a wider self, it quivers along various radii like the wind-rose on a compass, and the actual in it is continuously one with possibilities not yet in our present sight. And just as we are coconscious with our own momentary margin, may not we ourselves form the margin of some more really central self in things which is coconscious with the whole of us? May not you and I be confluent in a higher consciousness, and confluently active there, tho' we now know it not?[55]

"Thinking nonconceptually" means having access to

these wider energies; it means "giving up our own will and letting something higher work for us." Coming full circle back to the paradox of "not caring" and "doing it," of renunciation and action, the secret for James is the "new ranges of life succeeding upon our most despairing moments," opening up "possibilities that take our breath away, of another kind of happiness and power."

In our conversation with James, I have suggested that he, in effect, is making a radical distinction between two levels or even modes of self. The first and ordinary level of self is associated with conceptualism and intellectualism (as well as with emotion, at least in the usual sense), and it insists on its exclusive right to dominate and control. But life will "teach the lesson" and lead to the death of this self and the subsequent birth of a deeper second self, one that is sometimes identified as "will" in the writings of James. This second self is paradoxically both that aspect that is most intimately and truly myself, and at the same time the place in myself where I open onto or am confluent with the higher or wider vitalities of a pluralistic universe.

I have also suggested that in James it is not just "life" that "teaches the lesson" in a random way, but especially life as it is lived in the conversational relationship. It seems to me that for James the conversational relationship, the kind exemplified in the letter to his wife cited at the beginning of this essay, is the practice through which "the lesson" and revitalization occur. But James never quite says this directly. Perhaps his genius is that he *does* this without *saying* it, leaving it to his later conversation partners to make the point explicitly.

In his ordinary or ego self James may have felt disappointment in his later years about his failure to produce a "systematic" philosophy. But in his deeper self he lives on in a vitalizing conversation with us. I commend this conversation with William James to the reader, wishing you every good fruit of this splendid practice!

---

1 James, "Hegel and His Method," in *A Pluralistic Universe*, Cambridge, Harvard University Press, 1977, 44.

2 James, "On a Certain Blindness in Human Beings," in *Talks to Teachers on Psychology and to Students on Some of Life's Ideals* Cambridge, Harvard University Press, 1983, 149.

3 My colleague Kelly Parker, in conversation about an earlier draft of this introduction, points out that my thesis could be extended to argue that the American tradition itself is conversational: in its pre-twentieth-century stage, if James is its philosopher, then Emerson is the preacher, Whitman the poet, and Twain the conversational storyteller.

4 In a fuller treatment of James's work one could demonstrate how conversation is the organizing principle of each of his writings taken individually, as well as of his work overall.

5 Hannah Arendt, *The Human Condition*, Chicago: University of Chicago Press, 1958, 2–3. On the themes of return and the gift quality of life, see my *Leaving and Returning: On America's Contribution to a World Ethic*, Lewisburg, Pa., Bucknell University Press, 1989 and *Rediscovering the West: An Inquiry into Nothingness and Relatedness*, Albany, N.Y., SUNY Press, 1994.

6 James, "The Types of Philosophic Thinking," in *A Pluralistic Universe*, 11.

7 James, "The Gospel of Relaxation," in *Talks to Teachers*, 131.

8 Ibid., 127.

9 James, "On a Certain Blindness in Human Beings," 147.

10 James, "Conclusions," in *A Pluralistic Universe*, 138.

11 James, "The Continuity of Experience," in *A Pluralistic Universe*, 131.

[12] James, "Diary: April 30, 1870," in John J. McDermott, ed., *The Writings of William James*, Chicago, University of Chicago Press, 1977, 8.

[13] Ibid.

[14] James, "Conclusions," 137–8.

[15] James, "Types of Philosophic Thinking," 9.

[16] Ibid., 10.

[17] Ibid., 15.

[18] Ibid., 14.

[19] Ibid.

[20] Ibid., 12.

[21] Ibid., 11.

[22] James, "Conclusions," 143.

[23] James, "Types of Philosophic Thinking," 10–11.

[24] Ibid., 11.

[25] James, "The Moral Equivalent of War," in *Essays in Religion and Morality*, Cambridge, Harvard University Press, 1982, 165, 169.

[26] James, "The Will to Believe," in *The Will to Believe and Other Essays in Popular Philosophy*, Cambridge, Harvard University Press, 1979, 31.

[27] James, "What Pragmatism Means," in *Pragmatism*, Cambridge, Harvard University Press, 1975, 43–4.

[28] James, "The Continuity of Experience," 125.

[29] James, "Types of Philosophic Thinking," 17.

[30] Ibid., 19.

[31] Ibid., 21.

[32] James, "Conclusions," 145.

[33] James, "Hegel and His Method," 57.

34 Ibid.

35 James, "Monistic Idealism," in *A Pluralistic Universe*, 32.

36 James, "The Compounding of Consciousness," in *A Pluralistic Universe*, 99. My colleague Robert W. Mayberry points out that for further inquiry we should investigate the sense in which James himself is giving voice to a Platonism he does not recognize, because his criticisms of Plato appear to be unexamined repetitions of the conventional interpretations of the nineteenth century. In arguing this Mayberry cites Stanley Rosen, *The Question of Being: A Reversal of Heidegger*, New Haven, Yale University Press, 1993, especially p. 29. In defence of Plato, and the "newer reading of Plato" that Robert has championed, he suggests that conversation in James, according to my interpretation, is an instance of the true rhetoric as presented by Socrates in the *Phaedrus*.

37 James, "Bergson and His Critique of Intellectualism," in *A Pluralistic Universe*, 114.

38 I have looked through many James books, both primary and secondary, attempting to locate his use of this phrase. I could not find the reference. It remains in the text because I think he actually did use the phrase and because, in any case, unhealthy introspection (or subjectivism) was a problem with which he was quite familiar. See, for example, Gerald E. Myers, *William James: His Life and Thought*, New Haven, Yale University Press, 1986, especially pp. 48–53, on how James used philosophy and "acts of thought" rather than introspection.

39 Rowe, *Rediscovering the West*, 1.

40 John B. Cobb, Jr., *Beyond Dialogue: Toward a Mutual Transformation of Christianity and Buddhism*, Philadelphia, Fortress Press, 1982, 59.

41 For example, see Kitaro Nishida, *An Inquiry Into the Good*, trans. Masao Abe and Christopher Ives, New Haven, Yale University Press, 1990, xiii–xv, 13, 33, 52.

42 Ibid., xvii.

43 James, "The Dilemma of Determinism," in *The Will to Believe* 136–7.

44 Ira Progoff, *The Death and Rebirth of Psychology*, New York, McGraw-Hill, 1956, 3.

45 There are various intriguing references in James to meditation as a spiritual practice of this sort. See, for example, *Talks to Teachers*, p. 52, about the "daily exercise" of Hindus, and p. 147, about "a chieftain [saying] to his white guest, 'thou wilt never know the happiness of both thinking of nothing and doing nothing.' " Still, it is not clear to me that James himself entered into any spiritual practice in a self-conscious and disciplined way. In fact, there is some evidence that he maintained himself as an outsider, in a peculiar sort of twentieth-century asceticism (see my *Rediscovering the West*, 123–4). My suggestion in this essay, of course, is that the primary—though mostly unacknowledged (by himself as well as by his later commentators)—spiritual practice of James is conversation. It should also be observed that some of his experiences in the American wilderness (for example, see his letter to his wife at the beginning of this essay) have a distinctly meditative quality, though, again, they appear to be unacknowledged as such by James.

46 James, "The Stream of Consciousness," in *Psychology: Briefer Course* (Cambridge: Harvard University Press, 1984) 146–7. See also James's "A World of Pure Experience," "The Thing and Its Relations," and "The Place of Affectional Facts in a World of Pure Experience," in *Essays in Radical Empiricism* (Cambridge: Harvard University Press, 1976), 21–44, 45–59, 69–77. Clearly a major part of the significance of James lies in his rediscovery and articulation of an aspect of human experience that had been missing and/or radically downplayed in Western culture for some centuries. Whether James is recommending that this aspect is best spoken of as an "other" side—a "transitive" as opposed to "substantive" part of the stream of thought—or a deeper part (as is suggested by his talk of "descend[ing] to a more profound and primitive level") is not clear. These are questions that could be pursued in a more specialized study of James, including his relations with the various Hindus and Buddhists with whom he had contact.

47 James, "Psychology and the Teaching Art," in *Talks to Teachers*, 23–4.

48 James, "Bergson and His Critique of Individualism," 106.

49 Ibid.

50 James, "Continuity of Experience," 131.

51 James, "Bergson and His Critique of Intellectualism," 112.

52 Ibid., 113.

53 James, "Continuity of Experience," 131.

54 Ibid., 132.

55 Ibid., 131.

PART TWO
Selections from James's Writings

On A Certain Blindness in Human Beings

from *Talks to Students*

Hands off: neither the whole of truth nor the whole of good is revealed to any single observer, although each observer gains a partial superiority of insight from the peculiar position in which he stands.

(pp. 132–49)

Our judgements concerning the worth of things, big or little, depend on the *feelings* the things arouse in us. Where we judge a thing to be precious in consequence of the *idea* we frame of it, this is only because the idea is itself associated already with a feeling. If we were radically feelingless, and if ideas were the only things our mind could entertain, we should lose all our likes and dislikes at a stroke, and be unable to point to any one situation or experience in life more valuable or significant than any other.

Now the blindness in human beings of which this discourse will treat is the blindness with which we all are afflicted in regard to the feelings of creatures and people different from ourselves.

We are practical beings, each of us, with limited functions and duties to perform. Each is bound to feel intensely the importance of his own duties and the significance of the situations that call these forth. But this feeling is in each of us a vital secret, for sympathy with which we vainly look to others—the others are too much absorbed in their own vital secrets to take an interest in ours. Hence the stupidity and injustice of our opinions, so far as they deal with the significance of alien lives. Hence the falsity of our judgments, so far as they presume to decide in an absolute way on the value of other persons' conditions or ideals.

Take our dogs and ourselves, connected as we are by a tie more intimate than most ties in this world; and yet, outside of that tie of friendly fondness, how insensible, each of us, to all that makes life significant for the other!—we to the rapture of bones under hedges, or smells of trees and lamp-posts, they to the delights of literature and art. As you sit reading the most moving romance you ever fell upon, what sort of a judge is your fox-terrier of your behavior? With all his good will towards you, the nature of your conduct is absolutely excluded from his comprehension. To sit there like a senseless statue, when you might be taking him to walk and throwing sticks for him to catch! What queer disease is this that comes over you every day, of holding things and staring at them like that for hours together, paralyzed of motion and vacant of all conscious life? The African savages came nearer the truth; but they, too, missed it, when they gathered wonderingly round one of our American travellers who in the interior had just come into possession of a stray copy of the New York *Commercial*

Advertiser, and was devouring it column by column. When he got through, they offered him a high price for the mysterious object; and being asked for what they wanted it, they said: "For an eye-medicine"—that being the only reason they could conceive of for the protracted bath which he had given his eyes upon its surface.

The spectator's judgment is sure to miss the root of the matter and to possess no truth. The subject judged knows a part of the world of reality which the judging spectator fails to see, knows more whilst the spectator knows less; and wherever there is conflict of opinion and difference of vision, we are bound to believe that the truer side is the side that feels the more and not the side that feels the less.

Let me take a personal example of the kind that befalls each one of us daily.

Some years ago, whilst journeying in the mountains of North Carolina, I passed by a large number of "coves," as they call them there, or heads of small valleys between the hills, which had been newly cleared and planted. The impression on my mind was one of unmitigated squalor. The settler had in every case cut down the more manageable trees, and left their charred stumps standing. The larger trees he had girdled and killed, in order that their foliage should not cast a shade. He had then built a log cabin, plastering its chinks with clay, and had set up a tall zigzag rail fence around the scene of his havoc, to keep the pigs and cattle out. Finally, he had irregularly planted the intervals between the stumps and trees with Indian corn, which grew among the chips; and there he dwelt with his wife and babes—an axe, a gun, a few utensils, and some pigs and chickens feeding in the woods, being the sum total of his possessions.

The forest had been destroyed; and what had

"improved" it out of existence was hideous, a sort of ulcer, without a single element of artificial grace to make up for the loss of Nature's beauty. Ugly indeed seemed the life of the squatter, scudding, as the sailors say, under bare poles, beginning again away back where our first ancestors started, and by hardly a single item the better off for all the achievements of the intervening generations.

Talk about going back to Nature! I said to myself, oppressed by the dreariness, as I drove by. Talk of a country life for one's old age and for one's children! Never thus, with nothing but the bare ground and one's bare hands to fight the battle! Never, without the best spoils of culture woven in! The beauties and commodities gained by the centuries are sacred. They are our heritage and birth-right. No modern person ought to be willing to live a day in such a state of rudimentariness and denudation.

Then I said to the mountaineer who was driving me: "What sort of people are they who have to make these new clearings?" "All of us," he replied; "why, we ain't happy here unless we are getting one of these coves under cultivation." I instantly felt that I had been losing the whole inward significance of the situation. Because to me the clearings spoke of naught but denudation, I thought that to those whose sturdy arms and obedient axes had made them they could tell no other story. But when *they* looked on the hideous stumps, what they thought of was personal victory. The chips, the girdled trees and the vile split rails spoke of honest sweat, persistent toil and final reward. The cabin was a warrant of safety for self and wife and babes. In short, the clearing, which to me was a mere ugly picture on the retina, was to them a symbol redolent with moral memories and sang a very pæan of duty, struggle, and success.

I had been as blind to the peculiar ideality of their conditions as they certainly would also have been to the ideality of mine, had they had a peep at my strange indoor academic ways of life at Cambridge.

Wherever a process of life communicates an eagerness to him who lives it, there the life becomes genuinely significant. Sometimes the eagerness is more knit up with the motor activities, sometimes with the perceptions, sometimes with the imagination, sometimes with reflective thought. But wherever it is found, there is the zest, the tingle, the excitement, of reality; and there *is* "importance" in the only real and positive sense in which importance ever anywhere can be.

Robert Louis Stevenson has illustrated this by a case drawn from the sphere of the imagination, in an essay which I really think deserves to become immortal, both for the truth of its matter and the excellence of its form.

"Toward the end of September," Stevenson writes, "when school-time was drawing near and the nights were already black, we would begin to sally from our respective villas, each equipped with a tin bull's-eye lantern. The thing was so well known that it had worn a rut in the commerce of Great Britain; and the grocers, about the due time, began to garnish their windows with our particular brand of luminary. We wore them buckled to the waist upon a cricket belt, and over them, such was the rigour of the game, a buttoned top-coat. They smelled noisomely of blistered tin; they never burned aright, though they would always burn our fingers; their use was naught; the pleasure of them merely fanciful; and yet a boy with a bull's-eye under his top-coat asked for nothing more. The fishermen used lanterns about

their boats, and it was from them, I suppose, that we had
got the hint; but theirs were not bull's-eyes, nor did we ever
play at being fishermen. The police carried them at their
belts, and we had plainly copied them in that; yet we did
not pretend to be policemen. Burglars, indeed, we may have
had some haunting thoughts of; and we had certainly an eye
to past ages when lanterns were more common, and to certain story-books in which we had found them to figure very
largely. But take it for all in all, the pleasure of the thing was
substantive; and to be a boy with a bull's-eye under his top-
coat was good enough for us.

"When two of these asses met, there would be an
anxious 'Have you got your lantern?' and a gratified 'Yes!'
That was the shibboleth, and very needful too; for, as it
was the rule to keep our glory contained, none could
recognise a lantern-bearer, unless (like the pole-cat) by
the smell. Four or five would sometimes climb into the
belly of a ten-man lugger, with nothing but the thwarts
above them—for the cabin was usually locked, or choose
out some hollow of the links where the wind might
whistle overhead. There the coats would be unbuttoned
and the bull's-eyes discovered; and in the chequering
glimmer, under the huge windy hall of the night, and
cheered by a rich steam of toasting tinware, these fortunate young gentlemen would crouch together in the cold
sand of the links or on the scaly bilges of the fishing-
boat, and delight themselves with inappropriate talk.
Woe is me that I may not give some specimens. . . . But
the talk was but a condiment; and these gatherings themselves only accidents in the career of the lantern-bearer.
The essence of this bliss was to walk by yourself in the
black night; the slide shut, the top-coat buttoned; not a
ray escaping, whether to conduct your footsteps or to
make your glory public: a mere pillar of darkness in the

dark; and all the while, deep down in the privacy of your fool's heart, to know you had a bull's-eye at your belt, and to exult and sing over the knowledge.

"It is said that a poet has died young in the breast of the most stolid. It may be contended, rather, that this (somewhat minor) bard in almost every case survives, and is the spice of life to his possessor. Justice is not done to the versatility and the unplumbed childishness of man's imagination. His life from without may seem but a rude mound of mud; there will be some golden chamber at the heart of it, in which he dwells delighted; and for as dark as his pathway seems to the observer, he will have some kind of a bull's-eye at his belt.

". . . There is one fable that touches very near the quick of life: the fable of the monk who passed into the woods, heard a bird break into song, hearkened for a trill or two, and found himself on his return a stranger at his convent gates; for he had been absent fifty years, and of all his comrades there survived but one to recognise him. It is not only in the woods that this enchanter carols, though perhaps he is native there. He sings in the most doleful places. The miser hears him and chuckles, and the days are moments. With no more apparatus than an ill-smelling lantern I have evoked him on the naked links. All life that is not merely mechanical is spun out of two strands: seeking for that bird and hearing him. And it is just this that makes life so hard to value, and the delight of each so incommunicable. And just a knowledge of this, and a remembrance of those fortunate hours in which the bird *has* sung to *us*, that fills us with such wonder when we turn the pages of the realist. There, to be sure, we find a picture of life in so far as it consists of mud and of old iron, cheap desires and cheap fears, that which we are ashamed to remember and that which we are careless whether we forget; but of the note of that time-devouring nightingale we hear no news.

". . . Say that I came [in such a realistic romance] on some such business as that of my lantern-bearers on the links; and described the boys as very cold, spat upon by flurries of rain, and drearily surrounded, all of which they were; and their talk as silly and indecent, which it certainly was. . . . To the eye of the observer they *are* wet and cold and drearily surrounded; but ask themselves, and they are in the heaven of a recondite pleasure, the ground of which is an ill-smelling lantern.

"For, to repeat, the ground of a man's joy is often hard to hit. It may hinge at times upon a mere accessory, like the lantern, it may reside in the mysterious inwards of psychology. . . . It has so little bond with externals . . . that it may even touch them not; and the man's true life, for which he consents to live, lie altogether in the field of fancy. . . . In such a case the poetry runs underground. The observer (poor soul, with his documents!) is all abroad. For to look at the man is but to court deception. We shall see the trunk from which he draws his nourishment; but he himself is above and abroad in the green dome of foliage, hummed through by winds and nested in by nightingales. And the true realism were that of the poets, to climb up after him like a squirrel, and catch some glimpse of the heaven for which he lives. And the true realism, always and everywhere, is that of the poets: to find out where joy resides, and give it a voice far beyond singing.

"For to miss the joy is to miss all. In the joy of the actors lies the sense of any action. That is the explanation, that the excuse. To one who has not the secret of the lanterns, the scene upon the links is meaningless. And hence the haunting and truly spectral unreality of realistic books. . . . In each, we miss the personal poetry, the enchanted atmosphere, that rainbow work of fancy that clothes what is naked and seems to ennoble what is base; in each, life falls dead like dough, instead of soaring away like a balloon into the colours of the sunset; each is true, each inconceivable; for no man lives in the external truth, among salts and acids, but in the warm, phantasmagoric chamber of his brain, with the painted windows and the storied walls."[1]

These paragraphs are the best thing I know in all Stevenson.

"To miss the joy is to miss all." Indeed, it is. Yet we are but finite, and each one of us has some single specialized vocation of his own. And it seems as if energy in the service of its particular duties might be got only by hardening the heart towards everything unlike them. Our deadness towards all but one particular kind of joy would thus be the price we inevitably have to pay for being practical creatures. Only in some pitiful dreamer, some philosopher, poet, or romancer, or when the common practical man becomes a lover, does the hard externality give way, and a gleam of insight into the ejective world, as Clifford called it, the vast world of inner life beyond us, so different from that of outer seeming, illuminate our mind. Then the whole scheme of our customary values gets confounded, then our self is riven and its narrow interests fly to pieces, then a new centre and a new perspective must be found.

The change is well described by my colleague, Josiah Royce:

"What then is thy neighbor? Thou hast regarded his thought, his feeling, as somehow different from thine. Thou hast said: 'A pain in him is not like a pain in me, but something far easier to bear.' He seems to thee a little

less living than thou. His life is dim, it is cold, it is a pale
fire beside thy own burning desires. . . . So, dimly and by
instinct, thou hast lived with thy neighbor, and hast
known him not, being blind. Thou hast made [of him] a
thing, no Self at all. Have done with this illusion and simply try to know the truth. Pain is pain, joy is joy, everywhere even as in thee. In all the songs of the forest birds;
in all the cries of the wounded and dying, struggling in
the captor's power; in the boundless sea, where the myriads of water-creatures strive and die; amid all the count-
less hordes of savage men; in all sickness and sorrow; in
all exultation and hope; everywhere from the lowest to
the noblest, the same conscious, burning, willful life is
found, endlessly manifold as the forms of the living creatures, unquenchable as the fires of the sun, real as these
impulses that even now throb in thy own little selfish
heart. Lift up thy eyes, behold that life, and then turn
away and forget it as thou canst; but if thou has *known*
that, thou hast begun to know thy duty."[2]

This higher vision of an inner significance in what,
until then, we had realized only in the dead external
way, often comes over a person suddenly; and when it
does so, it makes an epoch in his history. As Emerson
says, there is a depth in those moments that constrains us
to ascribe more reality to them than to all other experiences. The passion of love will shake one like an explo-
sion, or some act will awaken a remorseful compunction
that hangs like a cloud over all one's later day.

This mystic sense of hidden meaning starts upon us
often from non-human natural things. I take this passage
from *Obermann*, a French novel that had some vogue in
its day: "Paris, March 7.—It was dark and rather cold. I
was gloomy, and walked because I had nothing to do. I
passed by some flowers placed breast-high upon a wall.

A jonquil in bloom was there. It is the strongest expression of desire: it was the first perfume of the year. I felt all the happiness destined for man. This unutterable harmony of souls, the phantom of the ideal world, arose in me complete. I never felt anything so great or so instantaneous. I know not what shape, what analogy, what secret of relation it was that made me see in this flower a limitless beauty. . . . I shall never enclose in a conception this power, this immensity that nothing will express; this form that nothing will contain; this ideal of a better world which one feels, but which it would seem that nature has not made."[3]

Wordsworth and Shelley are similarly full of this sense of a limitless significance in natural things. In Wordsworth it was a somewhat austere and moral significance, a 'lonely cheer.'

> To every natural form, rock, fruit or flower,
> Even the loose stones that cover the high-way,
> I gave a moral life: I saw them feel,
> Or linked them to some feeling: the great mass
> Lay bedded in a quickening soul, and all
> That I beheld respired with inward meaning.[4]

"Authentic tidings of invisible things!" Just what this hidden presence in Nature was, which Wordsworth so rapturously felt, and in the light of which he lived, tramping the hills for days together, the poet never could explain logically or in articulate conceptions. Yet to the reader who may himself have had gleaming moments of a similar sort the verses in which Wordsworth simply proclaims the fact of them come with a heart-satisfying authority:

                                        Magnificent
   The morning rose, in memorable pomp,
   Glorious as e'er I had beheld—in front,
   The sea lay laughing at a distance; near,
   The solid mountains shone, bright as the clouds,
   Grain-tinctured, drenched in empyrean light;
   And in the meadows and the lower grounds
   Was all the sweetness of a common dawn—
   Dews, vapours, and the melody of birds,
   And labourers going forth to till the fields.

   Ah! need I say, dear Friend! that to the brim
   My heart was full; I made no vows, but vows
   Were then made for me; bond unknown to me
   Was given, that I should be, else sinning greatly,
   A dedicated Spirit. On I walked
   In thankful blessedness, which yet survives.[5]

As Wordsworth walked, filled with his strange inner joy,
responsive thus to the secret life of Nature roundabout
him, his rural neighbors, tightly and narrowly intent upon
their own affairs, their crops and lambs and fences, must
have thought him a very insignificant and foolish person-
age. It surely never occurred to any one of them to wonder what was going on inside of *him* or what it might be
worth. And yet that inner life of his carried the burden of
a significance that has fed the souls of others, and fills
them to this day with inner joy.

   Richard Jefferies has written a remarkable autobio-
graphic document entitled *The Story of My Heart*. It tells,
in many pages, of the rapture with which in youth the
sense of the life of nature filled him. On a certain hill-
top, he says:

"I was utterly alone with the sun and the earth. Lying down on the grass, I spoke in my soul to the earth, the sun, the air, and the distant sea far beyond sight. . . . With all the intensity of feeling which exalted me, all the intense communion I held with the earth, the sun and sky, the stars hidden by the light, with the ocean—in no manner can the thrilling depth of these feelings be written—with these I prayed, as if they were the keys of an instrument. . . . The great sun burning with light; the strong earth, dear earth; the warm sky; the pure air; the thought of ocean; the inexpressible beauty of all filled me with a rapture, an ecstasy, an inflatus. With this inflatus, too, I prayed. . . . The prayer, this soul-emotion, was in itself, not for an object; it was a passion. I hid my face in the grass, I was wholly prostrated, I lost myself in the wrestle, I was rapt and carried away. . . . Had any shepherd accidentally seen me lying on the turf, he would only have thought that I was resting a few minutes. I made no outward show. Who could have imagined the whirlwind of passion that was going on within me as I reclined there!"[6]

Surely a worthless hour of life when measured by the usual standards of commercial value. Yet in what other *kind* of value can the preciousness of any hour, made precious by any standard, consist, if it consist not in feelings of excited significance like these, engendered in someone by what the hour contains?

Yet so blind and dead does the clamor of our own practical interests make us to all other things, that it seems almost as if it were necessary to become worthless as a practical being, if one is to hope to attain to any breadth of insight into the impersonal world of worths as such, to have any perception of life's meaning on a large

objective scale. Only your mystic, your dreamer, or your
insolvent tramp or loafer, can afford so sympathetic an
occupation, an occupation which will change the usual
standards of human values in the twinkling of an eye,
giving to foolishness a place ahead of power, and laying
low in a minute the distinctions which it takes a hard-
working conventional man a lifetime to build up. You
may be a prophet at this rate; but you cannot be a world-
ly success.

Walt Whitman, for instance, is accounted by many of
us a contemporary prophet. He abolishes the usual
human distinctions, brings all conventionalisms into solu-
tion, and loves and celebrates hardly any human attribut-
es save those elementary ones common to all members
of the race. For this he becomes a sort of ideal tramp, a
rider on omnibus-tops and ferry-boats, and, considered
either practically or academically, a worthless unproduc-
tive being. His verses are but ejaculations—things mostly
without subject or verb, a succession of interjections on
an immense scale. He felt the human crowd as rapturously as Wordsworth felt the mountains, felt it as an
overpoweringly significant presence, simply to absorb
one's mind in which should be business sufficient and
worthy to fill the days of a serious man. As he crosses
Brooklyn ferry, this is what he feels:

> Flood-tide below me! I watch you face to face;
> Clouds of the west! sun there half an hour high! I
>   see you also face to face.
> Crowds of men and women attired in the usual
>   costumes! how curious you are to me!
> On the ferry-boats, the hundreds and hundreds that
>   cross, returning home, are more curious to me
>   than you suppose;

And you that shall cross from shore to shore years
hence, are more to me, and more in my
meditations, than you might suppose.
Others will enter the gates of the ferry, and cross
from shore to shore;
Others will watch the run of the flood-tide;
Others will see the shipping of Manhattan north and
west, and the heights of Brooklyn to the south
and east;
Others will see the islands large and small;
Fifty years hence, others will see them as they cross,
the sun half an hour high;
A hundred years hence, or ever so many hundred
years hence, others will see them,
Will enjoy the sunset, the pouring in of the flood-
tide, the falling back to the sea of the ebb-tide.
It avails not, neither time or place—distance avails
not;
Just as you feel when you look on the river and sky,
so I felt;
Just as any of you is one of a living crowd, I was
one of a crowd;
Just as you are refresh'd by the gladness of the river
and the bright flow, I was refresh'd;
Just as you stand and lean on the rail, yet hurry with
the swift current, I stood, yet was hurried;
Just as you look on the numberless masts of ships,
and the thick-stem'd pipes of steamboats, I
look'd.
I too many and many a time cross'd the river, the
sun half an hour high;
I watched the Twelfth-month sea-gulls—I saw them
high in the air, floating with motionless wings,
oscillating their bodies,

I saw how the glistening yellow lit up parts of their
    bodies, and left the rest in strong shadow,
I saw the slow-wheeling circles, and the gradual
    edging toward the south.
Saw the white sails of schooners and sloops—saw
    the ships at anchor,
The sailors at work in the rigging, or out astride the
    spars,
The scallop-edged waves in the twilight, the ladled
    cups, the frolicsome crests and glistening,
The stretch afar growing dimmer and dimmer, the
    gray walls of the granite store-houses by the
    docks,
On the neighboring shore, the fires from the
    foundry chimneys burning high . . . into the
    night,
Casting their flicker of black . . . into the clefts of
    streets.
These, and all else, were to me the same as they are
    to you.[7]

And so on, through the rest of a divinely beautiful
poem. And if you wish to see what this hoary loafer considered the most worthy way of profiting by life's heaven-
sent opportunities, read the delicious volume of his letters
to a young car-conductor who had become his friend:

New York, Oct. 9, 1868.
    DEAR PETE. It is splendid here this forenoon—
bright and cool. I was out early taking a short walk
by the river only two squares from where I live. . . .
Shall I tell you about [my life] just to fill up? I generally spend the forenoon in my room writing, etc.,
then take a bath fix up and go out about 12 and

loafe somewhere or call on someone down town or on business, or perhaps if it is very pleasant and I feel like it ride a trip with some driver friend on Broadway from 23rd Street to Bowling Green, three miles each way. (Every day I find I have plenty to do, every hour is occupied with something.) You know it is a never ending amusement and study and recreation for me to ride a couple of hours of a pleasant afternoon on a Broadway stage in this way. You see everything as you pass, a sort of living, endless panorama—shops and splendid buildings and great windows: and on the broad sidewalks crowds of women richly dressed continually passing altogether different, superior in style and looks from any to be seen anywhere else—in fact a perfect stream of people—men too dressed in high style, and plenty of foreigners—and then in the streets the thick crowd of carriages, stages, carts, hotel and private coaches, and in fact all sorts of vehicles and many first class teams, mile after mile, and the splendor of such a great street and so many tall, ornamental, noble buildings many of them of white marble, and the gayety and motion on every side: you will not wonder how much attraction all this is on a fine day, to a great loafer like me, who enjoys so much seeing the busy world move by him, and exhibiting itself for his amusement, while he takes it easy and just looks on and observes.[8]

Truly a futile way of passing the time, some of you may say, and not altogether creditable to a grown-up man. And yet, from the deepest point of view, who knows the more of truth, and who knows the less—Whitman on his omnibus-top, full of the inner joy with

which the spectacle inspires him, or you, full of the disdain which the futility of his occupation excites?

When your ordinary Brooklynite or New Yorker,
leading a life replete with too much luxury, or tired and
careworn about his personal affairs, crosses the ferry or
goes up Broadway, *his* fancy does not thus 'soar away
into the colors of the sunset' as did Whitman's, nor does
he inwardly realize at all the indisputable fact that this
world never did anywhere or at any time contain more of
essential divinity, or of eternal meaning, than is embodied in the fields of vision over which his eyes so careless-
ly pass. There is life; and there, a step away, is death.
There is the only kind of beauty there ever was. There is
the old human struggle and its fruits together. There is
the text and the sermon, the real and the ideal in one.
But to the jaded and unquickened eye it is all dead and
common, pure vulgarism, flatness and disgust. "Hech! it
is a sad sight!" says Carlyle, walking at night with someone who appeals to him to note the splendor of the stars.
And that very repetition of the scene to new generations
of men *in secula seculorum*, that eternal recurrence of
the common order, which so fills a Whitman with mystic
satisfaction, is to a Schopenhauer, with the emotional
anæsthesia, the feeling of 'awful inner emptiness' from
out of which he views it all, the chief ingredient of the
tedium it instils. What is life on the largest scale, he asks,
but the same recurrent inanities, the same dog barking,
the same fly buzzing, forevermore? Yet of the kind of
fibre of which such inanities consist is the material
woven of all the excitements, joys and meanings that
ever were, or ever shall be, in this world.

To be rapt with satisfied attention, like Whitman, to
the mere spectacle of the world's presence, is one way,
and the most fundamental way, of confessing one's sense

of its unfathomable significance and importance. But how can one attain to the feeling of the vital significance of an experience, if one have it not to begin with? There is no receipt which one can follow. Being a secret and a mystery, it often comes in mysteriously unexpected ways. It blossoms sometimes from out of the very grave wherein we imagined that our happiness was buried. Benvenuto Cellini, after a life all in the outer sunshine, made of adventures and artistic excitements, suddenly finds himself cast into a dungeon in the Castle of San Angelo. The place is horrible. Rats and wet and mould possess it. His leg is broken; and his teeth fall out, apparently with scurvy. But his thoughts turn to God as they have never turned before. He gets a bible, which he reads during the one hour in the twenty-four in which a wandering ray of daylight penetrates his cavern; he has religious visions; he sings psalms to himself and composes hymns; and thinking, on the last day of July, of the festivities customary on the morrow in Rome, he says to himself: "All these past years I celebrated this holiday with the vanities of the world; from this year henceforward I will do it with the divinity of God. And then I said to myself, 'Oh, how much more happy I am for this present life of mine than for all those things remembered!'"[9]

But the great understander of these mysterious ebbs and flows is Tolstoi. They throb all through his novels. In his *War and Peace*, the hero, Peter, is supposed to be the richest man in the Russian empire. During the French invasion he is taken prisoner, and dragged through much of the retreat. Cold, vermin, hunger, and every form of misery assail him, the result being a revelation to him of the real scale of life's values. "Here only, and for the first time, he appreciated, because he was deprived of it, the happiness of eating when he was hungry, of drinking when he was thirsty, of sleeping when he was sleepy, and of talking when he felt the desire to exchange some words. . . . Later in life he always recurred with joy to this month of captivity, and never failed to speak with enthusiasm of the powerful and ineffaceable sensations, and especially of the moral calm, which he had experienced at this epoch. When at daybreak, on the morrow of his imprisonment, he saw [I abridge here Tolstoi's description] the mountains with their wooded slopes disappearing in the grayish mist; when he felt the cool breeze caress him; when he saw the light drive away the vapors, and the sun rise majestically behind the clouds and cupolas, and the crosses, the dew, the distance, the river, sparkle in the splendid, cheerful rays; his heart overflowed with emotion. This emotion kept continually with him, and increased a hundred-fold as the difficulties of his situation grew graver. . . . He learnt that man is meant for happiness, and that this happiness is in him, in the satisfaction of the daily needs of existence, and that unhappiness is the fatal result, not of our need, but of our abundance. . . . When calm reigned in the camp, and the embers paled and little by little went out, the full moon had reached the zenith. The woods and the fields roundabout lay clearly visible; and beyond the inundation of light which filled them, the view plunged into the limitless horizon. Then Peter cast his eyes upon the firmament, filled at that hour with myriads of stars. 'All that is mine,' he thought. 'All that is in me, is me! And that is what they think they have taken prisoner! That is what they have shut up in a cabin!'—So he smiled, and turned in to sleep among his comrades."[10]

The occasion and the experience, then, are nothing. It all depends on the capacity of the soul to be grasped, to have its life-currents absorbed by what is given.

"Crossing a bare common," says Emerson, "in snow puddles, at twilight, under a clouded sky, without having in my thoughts any occurrence of special good fortune, I have enjoyed a perfect exhilaration. I am glad to the brink of fear."

Life is always worth living if one have such responsive sensibilities. But we of the highly educated classes (so called) have most of us got far, far away from Nature. We are trained to seek the choice, the rare, the exquisite, exclusively, and to overlook the common. We are stuffed with abstract conceptions, and glib with verbalities and verbosities; and in the culture of these higher functions the peculiar sources of joy connected with our simpler functions often dry up, and we grow stone-blind and insensible to life's more elementary and general goods and joys.

The remedy under such conditions is to descend to a more profound and primitive level. To be imprisoned or shipwrecked or forced into the army would permanently show the good of life to many an over-educated pessimist. Living in the open air and on the ground, the lop-sided beam of the balance slowly rises to the level line; and the over-sensibilities and insensibilities even themselves out. The good of all the artificial schemes and fevers fades and pales; and that of seeing, smelling, tasting, sleeping, and daring and doing with one's body, grows and grows. The savages and children of nature to whom we deem ourselves so much superior, certainly are alive where we are often dead, along these lines; and could they write as glibly as we do, they would read us impressive lectures on our impatience for improvement and on our blindness to the fundamental static goods of life. "Ah, my brother," said a chieftain to his white guest, "thou wilt never know the happiness of both thinking of nothing and doing nothing; this, next to sleep, is the most enchanting of all things. Thus we were before our birth, and thus we shall be after death. Thy people, . . . when they have finished reaping one field, they begin to plough another, and as if the day were not enough, I have seen them plough by moonlight. What is their life to ours—their life that is as nought to them? Blind that they are, they lose it all! But we live in the present."[11]

The intense interest that life can assume when brought down to the non-thinking level, the level of pure sensorial perception, has been beautifully described by a man who *can* write, Mr. W. H. Hudson, in his volume, *Idle Days in Patagonia*.

"I spent the greater part of one winter," says this admirable author, "at a point on the Rio Negro, seventy or eighty miles from the sea. . . . It was my custom to go out every morning on horseback with my gun, and, followed by one dog, to ride away from the valley; and no sooner would I climb the terrace and plunge into the grey universal thicket, than I would find myself as completely alone as if five hundred instead of only five miles separated me from the valley and river. So wild and solitary and remote seemed that grey waste, stretching away into infinitude, a waste untrodden by man, and where the wild animals are so few that they have made no discoverable path in the wilderness of thorns. . . . Not once, nor twice, nor thrice, but day after day I returned to this solitude, going to it in the morning as if to attend a festival, and leaving it only when hunger and thirst and the westering sun compelled me. And yet I had no object in going—no motive which could be put into words; for although I carried a gun, there was nothing to shoot—the shooting was all left behind in the valley. . . . Sometimes I would pass an entire day without seeing one mammal, and perhaps not more than a dozen birds of any size. The weather at that time was cheerless, generally with a grey film of cloud spread over the sky, and a bleak wind, often cold enough to make my bridle hand quite numb. . . . At a slow pace, which would have seemed intolerable in other circumstances, I would ride about for hours at a stretch. On arriving at a hill, I would slowly ride to its summit, and stand there to survey the prospect. On every side it stretched away in great undulations, wild and irregular. How grey it all was! hardly less so near at hand than on the haze-wrapped horizon, where the hills were dim and the outline blurred by distance. Descending from my look-out, I would take up my aimless wanderings again, and visit other elevations to gaze on the same landscape from another point; and so on for hours, and at noon I would dismount and sit or lie on my folded poncho for an hour or longer. One day, in these rambles, I discovered a small grove composed of twenty to thirty trees, growing at a convenient distance apart, that had evidently been resorted to by a herd of deer or other wild animals. This grove was on a hill differing in shape from other hills in its neighbourhood; and after a time I made a point of finding and using it as a resting-place every day at noon. I did not ask myself why I made choice of that one spot, sometimes going miles out of my way to sit there, instead of sitting down under any one of the millions of trees and bushes on any other hillside. I thought nothing about it, but acted unconsciously; only afterwards it seemed to me that after having rested there once, each time I wished to rest again the wish came associated with the image of that particular clump of trees, with polished stems and clean bed of sand beneath; and in a short time I formed a habit of returning, animal-like, to repose at that same spot.

"It was perhaps a mistake to say that I would sit
down and rest, since I was never tired: and yet without
being tired, that noonday pause, during which I sat for
an hour without moving, was strangely grateful. All day
there would be no sound, not even the rustle of a leaf.
One day while *listening* to the silence, it occurred to my
mind to wonder what the effect would be if I were to
shout aloud. This seemed at the time a horrible suggestion, which almost made me shudder. But during those
solitary days it was a rare thing for any thought to cross
my mind. In the state of mind I was in, thought had
become impossible. My state was one of *suspense* and
watchfulness: yet I had no expectation of meeting with
an adventure, and felt as free from apprehension as I feel
now when sitting in a room in London. The state seemed
familiar rather than strange, and accompanied by a
strong feeling of elation; and I did not know that something had come between me and my intellect until I
returned to my former self—to thinking, and the old
insipid existence [again].

"I had undoubtedly *gone back*; and that state of
intense watchfulness, or alertness rather, with suspension
of the higher intellectual faculties, represented the mental
state of the pure savage. He thinks little, reasons little,
having a surer guide in his [mere sensory perceptions];
he is in perfect harmony with nature, and is nearly on a
level, mentally, with the wild animals he preys on, and
which in their turn sometimes prey on him."[12]

For the spectator, such hours as Mr. Hudson writes
of form a mere tale of emptiness, in which nothing happens, nothing is gained, and there is nothing to describe.
They are meaningless and vacant tracts of time. To him
who feels their inner secret, they tingle with an importance that unutterably vouches for itself. I am sorry for

the boy or girl, or man or woman, who has never been touched by the spell of this mysterious sensorial life, with its irrationality, if so you like to call it, but its vigilance and its supreme felicity. The holidays of life are its most vitally significant portions, because they are, or at least should be, covered with just this kind of magically irresponsible spell.

And now what is the result of all these considerations and quotations? It is negative in one sense, but positive in another. It absolutely forbids us to be forward in pronouncing on the meaninglessness of forms of existence other than our own; and it commands us to tolerate, respect, and indulge those whom we see harmlessly interested and happy in their own ways, however unintelligible these may be to us. Hands off: neither the whole of truth, nor the whole of good, is revealed to any single observer, although each observer gains a partial superiority of insight from the peculiar position in which he stands. Even prisons and sick-rooms have their special revelations. It is enough to ask of each of us that he should be faithful to his own opportunities and make the most of his own blessings, without presuming to regulate the rest of the vast field.

---

[1] "The Lantern-Bearers," in the volume entitled *Across the Plains*. Abridged in the quotation.

[2] *The Religious Aspect of Philosophy*, 1885, pp. 157–62 (abridged).

[3] De Sénancour, *Obermann*, Brussels, 1837, Lettre XXX.

[4] *The Prelude*, Book III.

[5] *The Prelude*, Book IV.

[6] *Op. cit.* Boston, Roberts, 1883, pp. 3, 4, 5, 6.

7 "Crossing Brooklyn Ferry" (abridged).

8 *Calamus*, Boston, 1897, pp. 41, 42.

9 *Vita*, lib. 2, chap. iv.

10 *La Guerre et la paix*, Paris, 1884, vol. 3, pp. 268, 275, 316.

11 Quoted by Lotze, *Microcosmus*, English translation, vol. 2, p. 240.

12 *Op. cit.*, pp. 210–222 (abridged).

The Gospel of Relaxation

from *Talks to Teachers*

The way to do it [that is, anything], paradoxical as it may seem, is genuinely not to care whether you are doing it or not. Then, possibly, by the grace of God, you may all at once find that you ARE doing it, and having learned what the trick feels like, you may (again by the grace of God) be enabled to go on.

(pp. 127–28)

Now from all this we can draw an extremely practical conclusion. If, namely, we wish our trains of ideation and volition to be copious and varied and effective, we must form the habit of freeing them from the inhibitive influence of reflection upon them, of egoistic preoccupation about their results. Such a habit, like other habits, can be formed. Prudence and duty and self-regard, emotions of ambition and emotions of anxiety, have, of course, a needful part to play in our lives. But confine them as far as possible to the occasions when you are making your general resolutions and deciding on your plans of campaign, and keep them out of the details.

When once a decision is reached and execution is the
order of the day, dismiss absolutely all responsibility and
care about the outcome. *Unclamp*, in a word, your intellectual and practical machinery, and let it run free; and
the service it will do you will be twice as good. Who are
the scholars who get 'rattled' in the recitation-room?
Those who think of the possibilities of failure and feel
the great importance of the act. Who are those who do
recite well? Often those who are most indifferent. *Their*
ideas reel themselves out of their memory of their own
accord. Why do we hear the complaint so often that
social life in New England is either less rich and expres-
sive or more fatiguing than it is in some other parts of
the world? To what is the fact, if fact it be, due unless to
the overactive conscience of the people, afraid of either
saying something too trivial and obvious, or something
insincere, or something unworthy of one's interlocutor,
or something in some way or other not adequate to the
occasion? How can conversation possibly steer itself
through such a sea of responsibilities and inhibitions as
this? On the other hand, conversation does flourish and
society is refreshing, and neither dull on the one hand
nor exhausting from its effort on the other, wherever
people forget their scruples and take the brakes off their
hearts, and let their tongues wag as automatically and
irresponsibly as they will.

They talk much in pædagogic circles to-day about
the duty of the teacher to prepare for every lesson in
advance. To some extent this is useful. But we Yankees
are assuredly not those to whom such a general doctrine
should be preached. We are only too careful as it is. The
advice I should give to most teachers would be in the
words of one who is herself an admirable teacher.
Prepare yourself in the *subject so well that it shall be*

always on tap; then in the class-room trust your spontaneity and fling away all farther care.

(p. 131)

The need of feeling responsible all the livelong day has been preached long enough in our New England. Long enough exclusively, at any rate—and long enough to the female sex. What our girl-students and woman-teachers most need nowadays is not the exacerbation, but rather the toning-down of their moral tensions. Even now I fear that some one of my fair hearers may be making an undying resolve to become strenuously relaxed, cost what it will, for the remainder of her life. It is needless to say that that is not the way to do it. The way to do it, paradoxical as it may seem, is genuinely not to care whether you are doing it or not. Then, possibly, by the grace of God, you may all at once find that you *are* doing it; and, having learned what the trick feels like, you may (again by the grace of God) be enabled to go on.

And that something like this may be the happy experience of all my hearers is, in closing, my most earnest wish.

Diary

from *The Letters of William James*

ed. by Henry James, Jr.,
Atlantic Monthly Press, Boston, 1920

(pp. 147–48)

April 30, 1870

"I think that yesterday was a crisis in my life. I finished
the first part of Renouvier's second 'Essais' and see no
reason why his definition of Free Will—'the sustaining of
a thought *because I choose to* when I might have other
thoughts'—need be the definition of an illusion. At any
rate, I will assume for the present—until next year—that
it is no illusion. My first act of free will shall be to believe
in free will. For the remainder of the year, I will abstain
from the mere speculation and contemplative *Grüblei* in
which my nature takes most delight, and voluntarily cul-
tivate the feeling of moral freedom, by reading books
favorable to it, as well as by acting. After the first of
January, my callow skin being somewhat fledged, I may
perhaps return to metaphysical study and skepticism
without danger to my powers of action. For the present
then remember: care little for speculation; much for the
form of my action; recollect that only when habits of

order are formed can we advance to really interesting fields of action—and consequently accumulate grain on grain of willful choice like a very miser; never forgetting how one link dropped undoes an indefinite number. *Principiis obsta*—Today has furnished the exceptionally passionate initiative which Bain posits as needful for the acquisition of habits. I will see to the sequel. Not in maxims, not in *Anschauungen*, but in accumulated *acts* of thought lies salvation. *Passer outre*. Hitherto, when I have felt like taking a free initiative, like daring to act originally, without carefully waiting for contemplation of the external world to determine all for me, suicide seemed the most manly form to put my daring into; now, I will go a step further with my will, not only act with it, but believe as well; believe in my individual reality and creative power. My belief, to be sure, *can't* be optimistic—but I will posit life (the real, the good) in the self-governing *resistance* of the ego to the world. Life shall [be built in] doing and suffering and creating."

The Types
of Philosophic
Thinking
from *A Pluralistic Universe*

> . . . all the parties are human beings with the same
> essential interests, and no one of them is the wholly
> perverse demon which another often imagines him
> to be. Both are loyal to the world that bears them;
> neither wishes to spoil it; neither wishes to regard it
> as an insane incoherence; both want to keep it as a
> universe of some kind; and their differences are all
> secondary to this deep agreement.

(pp. 14–23)

If we take the whole history of philosophy, the systems
reduce themselves to a few main types which, under all
the technical verbiage in which the ingenious intellect of
man envelopes them, are just so many visions, modes of
feeling the whole push, and seeing the whole drift of life,
forced on one by one's total character and experience,
and on the whole *preferred*—there is no other truthful

word—as one's best working attitude. Cynical characters take one general attitude, sympathetic characters another. But no general attitude is possible towards the world as a whole, until the intellect has developed considerable generalizing power and learned to take pleasure in synthetic formulas. The thought of very primitive men has hardly any tincture of philosophy. Nature can have little unity for savages. It is a *walpurgis-nacht* procession, a checkered play of light and shadow, a medley of impish and elfish friendly and inimical powers. 'Close to nature' tho' they live, they are anything but Wordsworthians. If a bit of cosmic emotion ever thrills them, it is likely to be at midnight, when the camp smoke rises straight to the wicked full moon in the zenith, and the forest is all whispering with witchery and danger. The eeriness of the world, the mischief and the manyness, the littleness of the forces, the magical surprises, the unaccountability of every agent, these surely are the characters most impressive at that stage of culture, these communicate the thrills of curiosity and the earliest intellectual stirrings. Tempests and conflagrations, pestilences and earthquakes, reveal supramundane powers, and instigate religious terror rather than philosophy. Nature, more demonic than divine, is above all things *multifarious*. So many creatures that feed or threaten, that help or crush, so many beings to hate or love, to understand or start at—which is on top and which subordinate? Who can tell? They are co-ordinate, rather, and to adapt ourselves to them singly, to "square" the dangerous powers and keep the others friendly, regardless of consistency or unity, is the chief problem. The symbol of nature at this stage, as Paulsen well says, is the sphinx, under whose nourishing breasts the tearing claws are visible.

But in due course of time the intellect awoke, with its passion for generalizing, simplifying and subordinating, and then began those divergences of conception which all later experience seems rather to have deepened than to have effaced, because objective nature has contributed to both sides impartially, and has let the thinkers emphasize different parts of her, and pile up opposite imaginary supplements.

Perhaps the most interesting opposition is that which results from the clash between what I lately called the sympathetic and the cynical temper. Materialistic and spiritualistic philosophies are the rival types that result: the former defining the world so as to leave man's soul upon it as a sort of outside passenger or alien, while the latter insists that the intimate and human must surround and underlie the brutal. This latter is the spiritual way of thinking.

Now there are two very distinct types or stages in spiritualistic philosophy, and my next purpose in this lecture is to make their contrast evident. Both types attain the sought-for intimacy of view, but the one attains it somewhat less successfully than the other.

The generic term spiritualism, which I began by using merely as the opposite of materialism, thus subdivides into two species, the more intimate one of which is monistic and the less intimate dualistic. The dualistic species is the *theism* that reached its elaboration in the scholastic philosophy, while the monistic species is the *pantheism* spoken of sometimes simply as idealism, and sometimes as "post-Kantian" or "absolute" idealism. Dualistic theism is professed as firmly as ever at all catholic seats of learning, whereas it has of late years tended to disappear at our british and american universities, and to be replaced by a monistic pantheism more or less open or disguised. I have an impression that ever since T. H. Green's time absolute idealism has been decidedly in the ascendent at Oxford. It is in the ascendent at my own university of Harvard.

Absolute idealism attains, I said, to the more intimate point of view; but the statement needs some explanation. So far as theism represents the world as God's world, and God as what Matthew Arnold called a magnified non-natural man, it would seem as if the inner quality of the world remained human, and as if our relations with it might be intimate enough—for what is best in ourselves appears then also outside of ourselves, and we and the universe are of the same spiritual species. So far, so good, then; and one might consequently ask, What more of intimacy do you require? To which the answer is that to be like a thing is not as intimate a relation as to be substantially fused into it, to form one continuous soul and body with it; and that pantheistic idealism, making us entitatively one with God, attains this higher reach of intimacy.

The theistic conception, picturing God and his creation as entities distinct from each other, still leaves the human subject outside of the deepest reality in the universe. God is from eternity complete, it says, and sufficient unto himself; he throws off the world by a free act and as an extraneous substance, and he throws off man as a third substance, extraneous to both the world and himself. Between them, God says "one", the world says "two", and man says "three"—that is the orthodox theistic view. And orthodox theism has been so jealous of God's glory that it has taken pains to exaggerate everything in the notion of him that could make for isolation and separateness. Page upon page in scholastic books go to prove that God is in no sense implicated by his

creative act, or involved in his creation. That his relation
to the creatures he has made should make any difference
to him, carry any consequence, or qualify his being, is
repudiated as a pantheistic slur upon his self-sufficingness. I said a moment ago that theism treats us and God
as of the same species, but from the orthodox point of
view that was a slip of language. God and his creatures
are *toto genere* distinct in the scholastic theology, they
have absolutely *nothing* in common; nay, it degrades
God to attribute to him any generic nature whatever; he
can be classed with nothing. There is a sense, then, in
which philosophic theism makes us outsiders and keeps
us foreigners in relation to God, in which, at any rate, his
connexion with us appears as unilateral and not reciprocal. His action can affect us, but he can never be affected
by our reaction. Our relation, in short, is not a strictly
social relation. Of course in common men's religion the
relation is believed to be social, but that is only one of
the many differences between religion and theology.

This essential dualism of the theistic view has all
sorts of collateral consequences. Man being an outsider
and a mere subject to God, not his intimate partner, a
character of externality invades the field. God is not heart
of our heart and reason of our reason, but our magistrate,
rather; and mechanically to obey his commands, however strange they may be, remains our only moral duty.
Conceptions of criminal law have in fact played a great
part in defining our relations with him. Our relations with
speculative truth show the same externality. One of our
duties is to know truth, and rationalist thinkers have
always assumed it to be our sovereign duty. But in
scholastic theism we find truth already instituted and
established without our help, complete apart from our
knowing; and the most we can do is to acknowledge it

passively and adhere to it, altho such adhesion as ours can make no jot of difference to what is adhered to. The situation here again is radically dualistic. It is not as if the world came to know itself, or God came to know himself, partly through us, as pantheistic idealists have maintained, but truth exists *per se* and absolutely, by God's grace and decree, no matter who of us knows it or is ignorant, and it would continue to exist unaltered, even tho' we finite knowers were all annihilated.

It has to be confessed that this dualism and lack of intimacy has always operated as a drag and handicap on Christian thought. Orthodox theology has had to wage a steady fight within the schools against the various forms of pantheistic heresy which the mystical experiences of religious persons, on the one hand, and the formal or aesthetic superiorities of monism to dualism, on the other, kept producing. God as intimate soul and reason of the universe has always seemed to some people a more worthy conception than God as external creator. So conceived, he appeared to unify the world more perfectly, he made it less finite and mechanical, and in comparison with such a God an external creator seemed more like the product of a childish fancy. I have been told by Hindoos that the great obstacle to the spread of Christianity in their country is the puerility of our dogma of creation. It has not sweep and infinity enough to meet the requirements of even the illiterate natives of India.

Assuredly most members of this audience are ready to side with Hinduism in this matter. Those of us who are sexagenarians have witnessed in our own persons one of those gradual mutations of intellectual climate, due to innumerable influences, that make the thought of a past generation seem as foreign to its successor as if it were the expression of a different race of men. The theological machinery that spoke so livingly to our ancestors, with its finite age of the world, its creation out of nothing, its juridical morality and eschatology, its relish for rewards and punishments, its treatment of God as an external contriver, an "intelligent and moral governor," sounds as odd to most of us as if it were some outlandish savage religion. The vaster vistas which scientific evolutionism has opened, and the rising tide of social democratic ideals, have changed the type of our imagination, and the older monarchical theism is obsolete or obsolescent. The place of the divine in the world must be more organic and intimate. An external creator and his institutions may still be verbally confessed at church in formulas that linger by their mere inertia, but the life is out of them, we avoid dwelling on them, the sincere heart of us is elsewhere.

I shall leave cynical materialism entirely out of our discussion as not calling for treatment before this present audience, and I shall ignore old-fashioned dualistic theism for the same reason. Our contemporary mind having once for all grasped the possibility of a more intimate *weltanschauung*, the only opinions quite worthy of arresting our attention will fall within the general scope of what may roughly be called the pantheistic field of vision, the vision of God as the indwelling divine rather than the external creator, and of human life as part and parcel of that deep reality.

As we have found that spiritualism in general breaks into a more intimate and a less intimate species, so the more intimate species itself breaks into two subspecies, of which the one is more monistic, the other more pluralistic in form. I say in form, for our vocabulary gets unmanageable if we don't distinguish between form and substance here. The inner life of things must be substantially akin anyhow to the tenderer parts of man's nature in any spiritualistic philosophy. The word 'intimacy' probably covers the essential difference. Materialism holds the foreign in things to be more primary and lasting, it sends us to a lonely corner with our intimacy. The brutal aspects overlap and outwear; refinement has the feebler and more ephemeral hold on reality.

From a pragmatic point of view the difference between living against a background of foreignness and one of intimacy means the difference between a general habit of wariness and one of trust. One might call it a social difference, for after all, the common *socius* of us all is the great universe whose children we are. If materialistic, we must be suspicious of this socius, cautious, tense, on guard. If spiritualistic, we may give way, embrace, and keep no ultimate fear.

The contrast is rough enough, and can be cut across by all sorts of other divisions, drawn from other points of view than that of foreignness and intimacy. We have so many different businesses with nature that no one of them yields us an all-embracing clasp. The philosophic attempt to define nature so that no one's business is left out, so that no one lies outside the door saying "Where do *I* come in?" is sure in advance to fail. The most a philosophy can hope for is not to lock out any interest forever. No matter what doors it closes, it must leave other doors open for the interests which it neglects. I have begun by shutting ourselves up to intimacy and foreignness because that makes so generally interesting a contrast, and because it will conveniently introduce a farther contrast to which I wish this hour to lead.

The majority of men are sympathetic. Comparatively few are cynics because they like cynicism, and most of our existing materialists are such because they think the evidence of facts impels them, or because they find the idealists they are in contact with too private and tender-minded; so, rather than join their company, they fly to the opposite extreme. I therefore propose to you to dis-regard materialists altogether for the present, and to con-sider the sympathetic party alone.

It is normal, I say, to be sympathetic in the sense in which I use the term. Not to demand intimate relations with the universe, and not to wish them satisfactory, should be accounted signs of something wrong. Accordingly when minds of this type reach the philo-sophic level, and seek some unification of their vision, they find themselves compelled to correct that aboriginal appearance of things by which savages are not troubled. That sphinx-like presence, with its breasts and claws, that first bald multifariousness, is too discrepant an object for philosophic contemplation. The intimacy and the for-eignness cannot be written down as simply co-existing. An order must be made; and in that order the higher side of things must dominate. The philosophy of the absolute agrees with the pluralistic philosophy which I am going to contrast with it in these lectures, in that both identify human substance with the divine substance. But whereas absolutism thinks that the said substance becomes fully divine only in the form of totality, and is not its real self in any form but the *all*-form, the pluralistic view which I prefer to adopt is willing to believe that there may ulti-mately never be an all-form at all, that the substance of reality may never get totally collected, that some of it may remain outside of the largest combination of it ever made, and that a distributive form of reality, the *each*-form, is logically as acceptable and empirically as proba-ble as the all-form commonly acquiesced in as so obviously the self-evident thing. The contrast between these two forms of a reality which we will agree to suppose substantially spiritual is practically the topic of this course of lectures. You see now what I mean by pantheism's two subspecies. If we give to the monistic subspecies the name of philosophy of the absolute, we may give that of radical empiricism to its pluralistic rival, and it may be well to distinguish them occasionally later by these names.

As a convenient way of entering into the study of their differences, I may refer to a recent article by Professor Jacks of Manchester College. Professor Jacks, in some brilliant pages in the *Hibbert Journal* for last October, studies the relation between the universe and the philosopher who describes and defines it for us. You may assume two cases, he says. Either what the philosopher tells us is extraneous to the universe he is accounting for, an indifferent parasitic outgrowth, so to speak; or the fact of his philosophizing is itself one of the things taken account of in the philosophy, and self-included in the description. In the former case the philosopher means by the universe everything *except* what his own presence brings; in the latter case his philosophy is itself an intimate part of the universe, and may be a part momentous enough to give a different turn to what the other parts signify. It may be a supreme reaction of the universe upon itself by which it rises to self-comprehension. It may handle itself differently in consequence of this event.

Now both empiricism and absolutism bring the philosopher inside and make man intimate, but the one being pluralistic and the other monistic, they do so in differing ways that need much explanation. Let me then contrast the one with the other way of representing the status of the human thinker.

For monism the world is no collection, but one great
all-inclusive fact outside of which is nothing—nothing is
its only alternative. When the monism is idealistic, this
all-enveloping fact is represented as an absolute mind
that makes the partial facts by thinking them, just as we
make objects in a dream by dreaming them, or person-
ages in a story by imagining them. To *be*, on this scheme,
is, on the part of a finite thing, to be an object for the
absolute; and on the part of the absolute it is to be the
thinker of that assemblage of objects. If we use the word
"content" here, we see that the absolute and the world
have an identical content. The absolute is nothing but the
knowledge of those objects; the objects are nothing but
what the absolute knows. The world and the all-thinker
thus compenetrate and soak each other up without
residuum. They are but two names for the same identical
material, considered now from the subjective, and now
from the objective point of view—*gedanke* and *gedacht-
es*, as we would say if we were Germans.

We philosophers naturally form part of the material,
on the monistic scheme. The absolute makes us by thinking us, and if we ourselves are enlightened enough to be
believers in the absolute, one may then say that our philosophizing is one of the ways in which the absolute is
conscious of itself. This is the full pantheistic scheme, the
identitätsphilosophie, the immanence of God in his creation, a conception sublime from its tremendous unity.
And yet that unity is incomplete, as a closer examination
will show.

The absolute and the world are one fact, I said,
when materially considered. Our philosophy, for example, is not numerically distinct from the absolute's own
knowledge of itself, not a duplicate and copy of it, it is
part of that very knowledge, is numerically identical with

as much of it as our thought covers. The absolute just *is* our philosophy, along with everything else that is known, in an act of knowing which (to use the words of my gifted absolutist colleague Royce) forms in its whole-ness one luminously transparent conscious moment.

But one as we are in this material sense with the absolute substance, that being only the whole of us, and we only the parts of it, yet in a formal sense something like a pluralism breaks out. When we speak of the absolute we *take* the one universal known material collectively or integrally; when we speak of its objects, of our finite selves, etc., we *take* that same identical material distributively and separately. But what is the use of a thing's *being* only once if it can be *taken* twice over, and if being taken in different ways makes different things true of it? As the absolute takes me, for example, I appear *with* everything else in its field of perfect knowledge. As I take myself, I appear *without* most other things in my field of relative ignorance. And practical differences result from its knowledge and my ignorance. Ignorance breeds mistake, curiosity, misfortune, pain, for me; I suffer those consequences. The absolute knows of those things, of course, for it knows me and my suffering, but it doesn't itself suffer. It can't be ignorant, for simultaneous with its knowledge of each question goes its knowledge of each answer. It can't be patient, for it has to wait for nothing, having everything at once in its possession. It can't be surprised; it can't be guilty. No attribute connected with succession can be applied to it, for it is all at once and wholly what it is, "with the unity of a single instant," and succession is not of it but in it, for we are continually told that it is "timeless."

Things true of the world in its finite aspects, then, are not true of it in its infinite capacity. *Quâ* finite and plural its accounts of itself to itself are different from what its account to itself *quâ* infinite and one must be.

With this radical discrepancy between the absolute and the relative points of view, it seems to me that almost as great a bar to intimacy between the divine and the human breaks out in pantheism as that which we found in monarchical theism, and hoped that pantheism might not show. We humans are incurably rooted in the temporal point of view. The eternal's ways are utterly unlike our ways. "Let us imitate the All" said the original prospectus of that admirable Chicago quarterly called the *Monist*. As if we could, either in thought or conduct! We are invincibly parts, let us talk as we will, and must always apprehend the absolute as if it were a foreign being. If what I mean by this is not wholly clear to you at this point, it ought to grow clearer as my lectures proceed.

The Continuity
of Experience

from *A Pluralistic Universe*

The return to life can't come about by talking. It is
an ACT; to make you return to life, I must set an
example for your imitation, I must deafen you to
talk, or to the importance of talk, by showing you,
as Bergson does, that the concepts we talk with are
made for purposes of PRACTICE and not for purposes of insight.

(pp. 129–32)

In *principle*, then, the real units of our immediately-felt
life are unlike the units that intellectualist logic holds to
and makes its calculations with. They are not separate
from their own others, and you have to take them at
widely separated dates to find any two of them that seem
unblent. Then indeed they do appear separate even as
their concepts are separate; a chasm yawns between
them; but the chasm itself is but an intellectualist fiction,
got by abstracting from the continuous sheet of experiences with which the intermediary time was filled. It is
like the log carried first by William and Henry, then by

William, Henry and John, then by Henry and John, then by John and Peter, and so on. All real units of experience *overlap*. Let a row of equidistant dots on a sheet of paper symbolize the concepts by which we intellectualize the world. Let a ruler long enough to cover at least three dots stand for our sensible experience. Then the conceived changes of the sensible experience can be symbolized by sliding the ruler along the line of dots. One concept after another will apply to it, one after another drop away, but it will always cover at least two of them, and no dots less than three will ever adequately cover *it*. You falsify it if you treat it conceptually, or by the law of dots.

What is true here of successive states must also be true of simultaneous characters. They also overlap each other with their being. My present field of consciousness is a centre surrounded by a fringe that shades insensibly into a subconscious more. I use three separate terms here to describe this fact; but I might as well use three hundred, for the fact is all shades and no boundaries. Which part of it properly is in my consciousness, which out? If I name what is out, it already has come in. The centre works in one way while the margins work in another, and presently overpower the centre and are central themselves. What we conceptually identify ourselves with and say we are thinking of at any time is the centre; but our *full* self is the whole field, with all those indefinitely radiating subconscious possibilities of increase that we can only feel without conceiving, and can hardly begin to analyze. The collective and the distributive ways of being coexist here, for each part functions distinctly, makes connexion with its own peculiar region in the still wider rest of experience and tends to draw us into that line, and yet the whole is somehow felt as one pulse of our life—not conceived so, but felt so.

In principle, then, as I said, intellectualism's edge is broken; it can only approximate to reality, and its logic is inapplicable to our inner life, which spurns its vetoes and mocks at its impossibilities. Every bit of us at every moment is part and parcel of a wider self, it quivers along various radii like the wind-rose on a compass, and the actual in it is continuously one with possibles not yet in our present sight.[1] And just as we are co-conscious with our own momentary margin, may not we ourselves form the margin of some more really central self in things which is co-conscious with the whole of us? May not you and I be confluent in a higher consciousness, and confluently active there, tho' we now know it not?

I am tiring myself and you, I know, by vainly seeking to describe by concepts and words what I say at the same time exceeds either conceptualization or verbalization. As long as one continues *talking*, intellectualism remains in undisturbed possession of the field. The return to life can't come about by talking. It is an *act*; to make you return to life, I must set an example for your imitation, I must deafen you to talk, or to the importance of talk, by showing you, as Bergson does, that the concepts we talk with are made for purposes of *practice* and not for purposes of insight. Or I must *point*, point to the mere *that* of life, and you by inner sympathy must fill out the *what* for yourselves. The minds of some of you, I know, will absolutely refuse to do so, refuse to think in non-conceptualized terms. I myself absolutely refused to do so for years together, even after I knew that the denial of manyness-in-oneness by intellectualism must be false, for the same reality does perform the most various functions at once. But I hoped ever for a revised intellectualist way round the difficulty, and it was only after reading Bergson that I saw that to continue using the intellectualist method was itself the fault. I saw that philosophy had been on a false scent ever since the days of Socrates and Plato, that an *intellectual* answer to the intellectualist's difficulties will never come, and that the real way out of them, far from consisting in the discovery of such an answer, consists in simply closing one's ears to the question. When conceptualism summons life to justify itself in conceptual terms, it is like a challenge addressed in a foreign language to someone who is absorbed in his own business; it is irrelevant to him altogether—he may let it lie unnoticed. I went thus through the "inner catastrophe" of which I spoke in the last lecture; I had literally come to the end of my conceptual stock-in-trade, I was bankrupt intellectualistically, and had to change my base. No words of mine will probably convert you, for words can be the names only of concepts. But if any of you try sincerely and pertinaciously on your own separate accounts to intellectualize reality, you may be similarly driven to a change of front. I say no more: I must leave life to teach the lesson.

---

1 The conscious self of the moment, the central self, is probably determined to this privileged position by its functional connexion with the body's imminent or present acts. It is the present *acting* self. Tho' the more that surrounds it may be 'subconscious' to us, yet if in its 'collective capacity' it also exerts an active function, it may be conscious in a wider way, conscious, as it were, over our heads.

On the relations of consciousness to action see Bergson's *Matière et mémoire, passim*, especially chap. i. Compare also the hints in Münsterberg's *Grundzüge der Psychologie*, chap. xv; those in my own *Principles of Psychology*, vol. ii, pp. 581–592; and those in W. McDougall's *Physiological Psychology*, chap. vii.

The Moral Equivalent of War

from *Essays in Religion and Morality*

But inordinate ambitions are the soul of every patriotism, and the possibility of violent death the soul of all romance. The militarily patriotic and romantic-minded everywhere, and especially the professional military class, refuse to admit for a moment that war may be a transitory phenomenon in social evolution. . . . So long as antimilitarists propose no substitute for war's disciplinary function, no moral equivalent of war, analogous, as one might say, to the mechanical equivalent of heat, so long they fail to realize the full inwardness of the situation.

(pp. 162–63)

The war against war is going to be no holiday excursion or camping party. The military feelings are too deeply grounded to abdicate their place among our ideals until better substitutes are offered than the glory and shame that come to nations as well as to individuals from the ups and downs of politics and the vicissitudes of trade. There is something highly paradoxical in the modern man's relation to war. Ask all our millions, north and south, whether they would vote now (were such a thing possible) to have our war for the Union expunged from history, and the record of a peaceful transition to the present time substituted for that of its marches and battles, and probably hardly a handful of eccentrics would say yes. Those ancestors, those efforts, those memories and legends, are the most ideal part of what we now own together, a sacred spiritual possession worth more than all the blood poured out. Yet ask those same people whether they would be willing in cold blood to start another civil war now to gain another similar possession, and not one man or woman would vote for the proposition. In modern eyes, precious tho' wars may be, they must not be waged solely for the sake of the ideal harvest. Only when forced upon one, only when an enemy's injustice leaves us no alternative, is a war now thought permissible.

It was not thus in ancient times. The earlier men were hunting men; and to hunt a neighboring tribe, kill the males, loot the village and possess the females, was the most profitable, as well as the most exciting, way of living. Thus were the more martial tribes selected, and in chiefs and peoples a pure pugnacity and love of glory came to mingle with the more fundamental appetite for plunder.

Modern war is so expensive that we feel trade to be a better avenue to plunder; but modern man inherits all the innate pugnacity and all the love of glory of his ancestors. To show war's irrationality and horror has no effect upon him. The horrors make the fascination. War is the *strong* life; it is life *in extremis*. War-taxes are the only ones men never hesitate to pay, as the budgets of all nations show.

History is a bath of blood. The Iliad is one long recital of how Diomedes and Ajax, Sarpedon and Hector *killed*. No detail of the wounds they made is spared us, and the Greek mind fed upon the story. Greek history is a panorama of jingoism and imperialism—war for war's sake, all the citizens being warriors. It is horrible reading, because of the irrationality of it all—save for the purpose of making 'history'—and the history is that of the utter ruin of a civilization which in intellectual respects was perhaps the highest the earth has ever seen.

(pp. 165–66)

In my remarks, pacificist tho' I am, I shall refuse to speak of the bestial side of the war-régime (already done justice to by so many writers) and consider only the higher aspects of militaristic sentiment. Patriotism no one thinks discreditable; nor does anyone deny that war is the romance of history. But inordinate ambitions are the soul of all patriotism, and the possibility of violent death the soul of all romance. The militarily patriotic and romantic-minded, and especially the professional military class, refuse to admit for a moment that war may be a transitory phenomenon in social evolution. The notion of a sheep's paradise like that revolts, they say, our higher imagination. Where then would be the steeps of life? If war had ever stopped, we should have to re-invent it, in their view, to redeem life from flat degeneration.

All reflective apologists for war at the present day take it religiously. It is to them a sort of sacrament; its profits are to the vanquished as well as to the victor; and quite apart from any question of profit, it is an absolute good, we are told, for it is human nature at its highest dynamic. Its "horrors" are a cheap price to pay for rescue from the only alternative supposed, of a world of clerks and teachers, of co-education and zoophily, of "consumers' leagues" and "associated charities," of industrialism unlimited, and feminism unabashed. No scorn, no hardness, no valor any more! Fie upon such a cattleyard of a planet!

So far as the central essence of this feeling goes, no healthy-minded person, it seems to me, can help partaking of it to some degree. Militarism is the great preserver of our ideals of hardihood, and human life without hardihood would be contemptible. Without risks or prizes for the darer, history would be insipid indeed; and there is a type of military character which everyone feels that the race should never cease to breed, for everyone is sensitive to its superiority. The duty is incumbent on mankind, of keeping military characters in stock—of keeping them, if not for use, then as ends in themselves and as pure pieces of perfection—so that Roosevelt's weaklings and mollycoddles may not end by making everything else disappear from the face of nature.

(pp. 168–69)

. . . mankind was nursed in pain and fear, and that the transition to a "pleasure-economy" may be fatal to a being untrained to powers of defence against its disintegrative influences. If we speak of *the fear of emancipation from the fear-régime*, we put the militarist attitude into a single phrase: fear regarding ourselves now taking the place of the ancient fear of the enemy.

Turn the fear over in my mind as I will, it all seems to lead back to two unwillingnesses of the imagination, one esthetic, and the other moral: unwillingness, first, to envisage a future in which army-life, with its many elements of charm, shall be forever impossible, and in which the destinies of peoples shall nevermore be decided quickly, thrillingly, and tragically by force, but only gradually and insipidly by "evolution"; and, secondly, unwillingness to see the supreme theatre of human strenuousness closed, and the splendid military aptitudes of men doomed to remain always in a state of latency and never to show themselves in action. These insistent unwillingnesses, no less than other esthetic and ethical insistencies, have, it seems to me, to be listened to and respected. One cannot meet them effectively by mere counter-insistency on war's expensiveness and horror. The horror makes the thrill; and when it is a question of getting the extremest and supremest out of human nature, talk of expense sounds ignominious. The weakness of so much merely negative criticism is evident—pacificism makes no converts from the military party. The military party denies neither the bestiality nor the horror, nor the expense; it only says that these things tell but half the story. It only says that war is *worth* these things; that, taking human nature as a whole, wars are its best protection against its weaker and more cowardly self, and that mankind cannot afford to adopt a peace-economy.

Pacificists ought to enter more deeply into the esthetical and ethical point of view of their opponents. Do that first in any controversy, says J. J. Chapman, *then move the point*, and your opponent will follow. So long as anti-militarists propose no substitutes for the disciplinary function of war, no *moral equivalent* of war, analogous, as one might say, to the mechanical equivalent of heat, so long they fail to realize the full inwardness of the situation. And as a rule they do fail. The duties, penalties and sanctions pictured in the utopias they paint are all too weak and tame to touch the military-minded. Tolstoy's pacificism is the only exception to this rule, for it is profoundly pessimistic as regards all this world's values, and makes the fear of the Lord furnish the moral spur provided elsewhere by the fear of the enemy. But our socialistic peace-advocates all believe absolutely in this world's values; and instead of the fear of the Lord and the fear of the enemy, the only fear they reckon with is the fear of poverty if one be lazy. This weakness pervades all the socialistic literature with which I am acquainted. Even in Lowes Dickinson's exquisite dialogue, high wages and short hours are the only forces invoked for overcoming man's distaste for repulsive kinds of labor. Meanwhile men at large still live as they always have lived, under a pain-and-fear economy—for those of us who live in an ease-economy are but an island in the stormy ocean—and the whole atmosphere of present-day utopian literature tastes mawkish and dishwatery to people who still keep a sense for life's more bitter flavors. It suggests, in truth, ubiquitous inferiority.

The Will to Believe
address to the
Philosophical Clubs of Yale
and Brown Universities
New World, June, 1896

. . . one who would shut himself up in snarling logicality and try to make the gods extort his recognition
willy-nilly, or not get it at all, might cut himself off
forever from his only opportunity to make the gods'
acquaintance. This feeling, forced on us we know
not whence, that by obstinately believing that there
are gods (although not to do so would be so easy
both for our logic and our life) we are doing the
universe the deepest service we can, seems part of
the living essence of the religious hypothesis.

In truths dependent on our personal action, then, faith
based on desire is certainly a lawful and possibly an
indispensable thing.

But now, it will be said, these are all childish human
cases, and have nothing to do with great cosmical matters, like the question of religious faith. Let us then pass
on to that. Religions differ so much in their accidents that
in discussing the religious question we must make it very

generic and broad. What then do we now mean by the religious hypothesis? Science says things are; morality says some things are better than other things; and religion says essentially two things.

First, she says that the best things are the more eternal things, the overlapping things, the things in the universe that throw the last stone, so to speak, and say the final word. "Perfection is eternal"—this phrase of Charles Secrétan seems a good way of putting this first affirmation of religion, an affirmation which obviously cannot yet be verified scientifically at all.

The second affirmation of religion is that we are better off even now if we believe her first affirmation to be true.

Now let us consider what the logical elements of this situation are *in case the religious hypothesis in both its branches be really true.* (Of course, we must admit that possibility at the outset. If we are to discuss the question at all, it must involve a living option. If for any of you religion be a hypothesis that cannot, by any living possibility be true, then you need go no farther. I speak to the "saving remnant" alone.) So proceeding, we see, first, that religion offers itself as a *momentous* option. We are supposed to gain, even now, by our belief, and to lose by our non-belief, a certain vital good. Secondly, religion is a *forced* option, so far as that good goes. We cannot escape the issue by remaining sceptical and waiting for more light, because, although we do avoid error in that way *if religion be untrue*, we lose the good, *if it be true*, just as certainly as if we positively chose to disbelieve. It is as if a man should hesitate indefinitely to ask a certain woman to marry him because he was not perfectly sure that she would prove an angel after he brought her home. Would he not cut himself off from that particular angel-possibility as decisively as if he went and married someone else? Scepticism, then, is not avoidance of option; it is option of a certain particular kind of risk. *Better risk loss of truth than chance of error*—that is your faith-vetoer's exact position. He is actively playing his stake as much as the believer is; he is backing the field against the religious hypothesis, just as the believer is backing the religious hypothesis against the field. To preach scepticism to us as a duty until "sufficient evidence" for religion be found, is tantamount therefore to telling us, when in presence of the religious hypothesis, that to yield to our fear of its being error is wiser and better than to yield to our hope that it may be true. It is not intellect against all passions, then; it is only intellect with one passion laying down its law. And by what, forsooth, is the supreme wisdom of this passion warranted? Dupery for dupery, what proof is there that dupery through hope is so much worse than dupery through fear? I, for one, can see no proof; and I simply refuse obedience to the scientist's command to imitate his kind of option, in a case where my own stake is important enough to give me the right to choose my own form of risk. If religion be true and the evidence for it be still insufficient, I do not wish, by putting your extinguisher upon my nature (which feels to me as if it had after all some business in this matter), to forfeit my sole chance in life of getting upon the winning side—that chance depending, of course, on my willingness to run the risk of acting as if my passional need of taking the world religiously might be prophetic and right.

All this is on the supposition that it really may be prophetic and right, and that, even to us who are discussing the matter, religion is a live hypothesis which may be true. Now to most of us religion comes in a still farther way that makes a veto on our active faith even more illogical. The more perfect and more eternal aspect of the universe is represented in our religions as having personal form. The universe is no longer a mere *It* to us, but a *Thou*, if we are religious; and any relation that may be possible from person to person might be possible here. For instance, although in one sense we are passive portions of the universe, in another we show a curious autonomy, as if we were small active centres on our own account. We feel, too, as if the appeal of religion to us were made to our own active good-will, as if evidence might be forever withheld from us unless we met the hypothesis half-way. To take a trivial illustration: just as a man who in a company of gentlemen made no advances, asked a warrant for every concession, and believed no one's word without proof, would cut himself off by such churlishness from all the social rewards that a more trust-ing spirit would earn—so here, one who should shut himself up in snarling logicality and try to make the gods extort his recognition willy-nilly, or not get it at all, might cut himself off forever from his only opportunity of mak-ing the gods' acquaintance. This feeling, forced on us we know not whence, that by obstinately believing that there are gods (although not to do so would be so easy both for our logic and our life) we are doing the universe the deepest service we can, seems part of the living essence of the religious hypothesis. If the hypothesis *were* true in all its parts, including this one, then pure intellectualism, with its veto on our making willing advances, would be an absurdity; and some participation of our sympathetic nature would be logically required. I, therefore, for one, cannot see my way to accepting the agnostic rules for truth-seeking, or wilfully agree to keep my willing nature out of the game. I cannot do so for this plain reason, that *a rule of thinking which would absolutely prevent me from acknowledging certain kinds of truth if those kinds of truth were really there, would be an irrational rule.* That for me is the long and short of the formal logic of the situation, no matter what the kinds of truth might materially be.

I confess I do not see how this logic can be escaped. But sad experience makes me fear that some of you may still shrink from radically saying with me, *in abstracto,* that we have the right to believe at our own risk any hypothesis that is live enough to tempt our will. I suspect, however, that if this is so, it is because you have got away from the abstract logical point of view altogether, and are thinking (perhaps without realizing it) of some particular religious hypothesis which for you is dead. The freedom to "believe what we will" you apply to the case of some patent superstition; and the faith you think of is the faith defined by the schoolboy when he said, "Faith is when you believe something that you know ain't true." I can only repeat that this is misapprehension. *In concreto,* the freedom to believe can only cover living options which the intellect of the individual cannot by itself resolve; and living options never seem absurdities to him who has them to consider. When I look at the religious question as it really puts itself to concrete men, and when I think of all the possibilities which both practically and theoretically it involves, then this command that we shall put a stopper on our heart, instincts and courage, and *wait*—acting of course meanwhile more or less as if religion were *not* true[1]—till doomsday, or till such time as our intellect and senses working together may have raked in evidence enough— this command, I say, seems to me the queerest idol ever manufactured in the philosophic cave. Were we scholastic absolutists, there might be more excuse. If we had an infallible intellect with its objective certitudes, we might feel ourselves disloyal to such a perfect organ of knowledge in not trusting to it exclusively, in not waiting for its releasing word. But if we are empiricists, if we believe that no bell in us tolls to let us know for certain when truth is in our grasp, then it seems a piece of idle fantasticality to preach so solemnly our duty of waiting for the bell. Indeed we *may* wait if we will—I hope you do not think that I am denying that—but if we do so, we do so at our peril as much as if we believed. In either case we *act*, taking our life in our hands. No one of us ought to issue vetoes to the other, nor should we bandy words of abuse. We ought, on the contrary, delicately and profoundly to respect one another's mental freedom—then only shall we bring about the intellectual republic; then only shall we have that spirit of inner tolerance without which all our outer tolerance is soulless, and which is empiricism's glory; then only shall we live and let live, in speculative as well as in practical things.

I began by a reference to Fitzjames Stephen; let me end by a quotation from him. "What do you think of yourself? What do you think of the world? . . . These are questions with which all must deal as it seems good to them. They are riddles of the Sphinx, and in some way or other we must deal with them. . . . In all important transactions of life we have to take a leap in the dark. . . . If we decide to leave the riddles unanswered, that is a choice. If we waver in our answer, that too is a choice; but whatever choice we make, we make it at our peril. If a man chooses to turn his back altogether on God and the future, no one can prevent him. No one can show beyond reasonable doubt that he is mistaken. If a man thinks otherwise, and acts as he thinks, I do not see how any one can prove that *he* is mistaken. Each must act as he thinks best, and if he is wrong so much the worse for him. We stand on a mountain pass in the midst of whirling snow and blinding mist, through which we get glimpses now and then of paths which may be deceptive. If we stand still, we shall be frozen to death. If we take the wrong road, we shall be dashed to pieces. We do not certainly know whether there is any right one. What must we do? 'Be strong and of a good courage.' Act for the best, hope for the best, and take what comes. . . . If death ends all, we cannot meet death better."[2]

---

[1] Since belief is measured by action, he who forbids us to believe religion to be true, necessarily also forbids us to act as we should if we did believe it to be true. The whole defence of religious faith hinges upon action. If the action required or inspired by the religious hypothesis is in no way different from that dictated by the naturalistic hypothesis, then religious faith is a pure superfluity, better pruned away, and controversy about its legitimacy is a piece of idle trifling, unworthy of serious minds. I myself believe, of course, that the religious hypothesis gives to the world an expression which specifically determines our reactions, and makes them in a large part unlike what they might be on a purely naturalistic scheme of belief.

[2] *Liberty, Equality, Fraternity*, p. 353, 2d edition. London, 1874.

What Pragmatism Means

from *Pragmatism*

You see by this what I meant when I called Pragmatism a mediator and reconciler and said, borrowing the word from Papini, that she "unstiffens" our theories. She has in fact no prejudices whatever, no obstructive dogmas, no rigid canons of what shall count as proof. She is completely genial. She will entertain any hypothesis, she will consider any evidence. . . . Her manners are as various and flexible, her resources as rich and various, and her conclusions as friendly as those of mother nature.

(pp. 43–44)

I said just now that what is better for us to believe is true *unless the belief incidentally clashes with some other vital benefit*. Now in real life what vital benefits is any particular belief of ours most liable to clash with? What indeed except the vital benefits yielded by *other beliefs* when these prove incompatible with the first ones? In other words, the greatest enemy of any one of our truths may be the rest of our truths. Truths have once for all this desperate instinct of self-preservation and of desire to extinguish whatever contradicts them. My belief in the Absolute, based on the good it does me, must run the gauntlet of all my other beliefs. Grant that it may be true in giving me a moral holiday. Nevertheless, as I conceive it,—and let me speak now confidentially, as it were, and merely in my own private person,—it clashes with other truths of mine whose benefits I hate to give up on its account. It happens to be associated with a kind of logic of which I am the enemy, I find that it entangles me in metaphysical paradoxes that are inacceptable, etc., etc. But as I have enough trouble in life already without adding the trouble of carrying these intellectual inconsistencies, I personally just give up the Absolute. I just *take* my moral holidays; or else as a professional philosopher, I try to justify them by some other principle.

If I could restrict my notion of the Absolute to its bare holiday-giving value, it wouldn't clash with my other truths. But we cannot easily thus restrict our hypotheses. They carry supernumerary features, and these it is that clash so. My disbelief in the Absolute means then disbelief in those other supernumerary features, for I fully believe in the legitimacy of taking moral holidays.

You see by this what I meant when I called pragmatism a mediator and reconciler and said, borrowing the word from Papini, that she "unstiffens" our theories. She has in fact no prejudices whatever, no obstructive dogmas, no rigid canons of what shall count as proof. She is completely genial. She will entertain any hypothesis, she will consider any evidence. It follows that in the religious field she is at a great advantage both over positivistic empiricism, with its anti-theological bias, and over religious rationalism, with its exclusive interest in the remote, the noble, the simple, and the abstract in the way of conception.

In short, she widens the field of search for God. Rationalism sticks to logic and the empyrean. Empiricism sticks to the external senses. Pragmatism is willing to take anything, to follow either logic or the senses, and to count the humblest and most personal experiences. She will count mystical experiences if they have practical consequences. She will take a God who lives in the very dirt of private fact—if that should seem a likely place to find him.

Her only test of probable truth is what works best in the way of leading us, what fits every part of life best and combines with the collectivity of experience's demands, nothing being omitted. If theological ideas should do this, if the notion of God, in particular, should prove to do it, how could pragmatism possibly deny God's existence? She could see no meaning in treating as "not true" a notion that was pragmatically so successful. What other kind of truth could there be, for her, than all this agreement with concrete reality?

In my last lecture I shall return again to the relations of pragmatism with religion. But you see already how democratic she is. Her manners are as various and flexible, her resources as rich and endless, and her conclusions as friendly as those of mother nature.

The Stream of Consciousness

from *Psychology: Briefer Course*

Now it is very difficult, introspectively, to see the transitive parts for what they really are. If they are but flights to a conclusion, stopping them to look at them before the conclusion is reached is really annihilating them. . . . The attempt at introspective analysis in these cases is in fact like seizing a spinning top to catch its motion, or trying to turn up the gas quickly enough to see how the darkness looks.

(pp. 146–48)

When we take a general view of the wonderful stream of our consciousness, what strikes us first is the different pace of its parts. Like a bird's life, it seems to be an alternation of flights and perchings. The rhythm of language expresses this, where every thought is expressed in a sentence, and every sentence closed by a period. The resting-places are usually occupied by sensorial imaginations of some sort, whose peculiarity is that they can be held before the mind for an indefinite time, and contemplated without changing; the places of flight are filled with thoughts of relations, static or dynamic, that for the most part obtain between the matters contemplated in the periods of comparative rest.

Let us call the resting-places the "substantive parts," and the places of flight the 'transitive parts,' of the stream of thought. It then appears that our thinking tends at all times towards some other substantive part than the one from which it has just been dislodged. And we may say that the main use of the transitive parts is to lead us from one substantive conclusion to another.

Now it is very difficult, introspectively, to see the transitive parts for what they really are. If they are but flights to a conclusion, stopping them to look at them before the conclusion is reached is really annihilating them. Whilst if we wait till the conclusion *be* reached, it so exceeds them in vigor and stability that it quite eclipses and swallows them up in its glare. Let anyone try to cut a thought across in the middle and get a look at its section, and he will see how difficult the introspective observation of the transitive tracts is. The rush of the thought is so headlong that it almost always brings us up at the conclusion before we can arrest it. Or if our purpose is nimble enough and we do arrest it, it ceases forthwith to be itself. As a snowflake caught in the warm hand is no longer a flake but a drop, so, instead of catching the feeling of relation moving to its term, we find we have caught some substantive thing, usually the last word we were pronouncing, statically taken, and with its function, tendency, and particular meaning in the sentence quite evaporated. The attempt at introspective analysis in these cases is in fact like seizing a spinning top to catch its motion, or trying to turn up the gas quickly enough to see how the darkness looks. And the challenge to *produce* these transitive states of consciousness, which is sure to be thrown by doubting psychologists at anyone who contends for their existence, is as unfair as Zeno's treatment of the advocates of motion, when, asking them to point out in what place an arrow *is* when it moves, he argues the falsity of their thesis from their inability to make to so preposterous a question an immediate reply.

The results of this introspective difficulty are baleful. If to hold fast and observe the transitive parts of thought's stream be so hard, then the great blunder to which all schools are liable must be the failure to register them, and the undue emphasizing of the more substantive parts of the stream. Now the blunder has historically worked in two ways. One set of thinkers have been led by it to *Sensationalism*. Unable to lay their hands on any substantive feelings corresponding to the innumerable relations and forms of connection between the sensible things of the world, finding no *named* mental states mirroring such relations, they have for the most part denied that any such states exist; and many of them, like Hume, have gone on to deny the reality of most relations *out* of the mind as well as in it. Simple substantive "ideas," sensations and their copies, juxtaposed like dominoes in a game, but really separate, everything else verbal illusion,—such is the upshot of this view. The *Intellectualists*, on the other hand, unable to give up the reality of relations *extra mentem*, but equally unable to point to any distinct substantive feelings in which they were known, have made the same admission that such feelings do not exist. But they have drawn an opposite conclusion. The relations must be known, they say, in something that is no feeling, no mental "state," continuous and consubstantial with the subjective tissue out of which sensations and other substantive conditions of consciousness are made. They must be known by something that lies on an entirely different plane, by an *actus purus* of Thought, Intellect, or Reason, all written with capitals and considered to mean something unutterably superior to any passing perishing fact of sensibility whatever.

But from our point of view both Intellectualists and Sensationalists are wrong. If there be such things as feelings at all, *then so surely as relations between objects exist* in rerum naturâ, *so surely, and more surely, do feelings exist to which these relations are known*. There is not a conjunction or a preposition, and hardly an adverbial phrase, syntactic form, or inflection of voice, in human speech, that does not express some shading or other of relation which we at some moment actually feel to exist between the larger objects of our thought. If we speak objectively, it is the real relations that appear revealed; if we speak subjectively, it is the stream of consciousness that matches each of them by an inward coloring of its own. In either case the relations are numberless, and no existing language is capable of doing justice to all their shades.

Psychology and the Teaching Art

from *Talks to Teachers*

. . . sciences never generate arts directly out of themselves. An intermediary inventive mind must make the application, by using its originality. . . . A science only lays down lines within which the rule of the art must fall, laws which the follower of the art must not transgress; but what particular thing he shall positively do within those lines is left exclusively to his own genius.

(pp. 15–16)

As regards this subject of psychology, now, I wish at the very threshold to do what I can to dispel the mystification. So I say at once that in my humble opinion there *is* no "new psychology" worthy of the name. There is nothing but the old psychology which began in Locke's time, plus a little physiology of the brain and senses and theory of evolution, and a few refinements of introspective detail, for the most part without adaptation to the teacher's use. It is only the fundamental conceptions of psychology which are of real value to the teacher; and they, apart from the aforesaid theory of evolution, are very far from being new—I trust that you will see better what I mean by this at the end of all these talks.

I say moreover that you make a great, a very great mistake, if you think that psychology, being the science of the mind's laws, is something from which you can deduce definite programmes and schemes and methods of instruction for immediate school-room use. Psychology is a science, and teaching is an art; and sciences never generate arts directly out of themselves. An intermediary inventive mind must make the application, by using its originality.

The science of logic never made a man reason rightly, and the science of ethics (if there be such a thing) never made a man behave rightly. The most such sciences can do is to help us to catch ourselves up and check ourselves, if we start to reason or to behave wrongly; and to criticise ourselves more articulately after we have made mistakes. A science only lays down lines within which the rules of the art must fall, laws which the follower of the art must not transgress; but what particular thing he shall positively do within those lines is left exclusively to his own genius. One genius will do his work well and succeed in one way, whilst another succeeds as well quite differently; yet neither will transgress the lines.

The art of teaching grew up in the school-room, out of inventiveness and sympathetic concrete observation. Even where (as in the case of Herbart) the advancer of the art was also a psychologist, the pædagogics and the psychology ran side by side, and the former was not derived in any sense from the latter. The two were congruent, but neither was subordinate. And so everywhere the teaching must *agree* with the psychology, but need not necessarily be the only kind of teaching that would so agree; for many diverse methods of teaching may equally well agree with psychological laws.

To know psychology, therefore, is absolutely no guarantee that we shall be good teachers. To advance to that result we must have an additional endowment altogether, a happy tact and ingenuity to tell us what definite things to say and do when the pupil is before us. That ingenuity in meeting and pursuing the pupil, that tact for the concrete situation, though they are the alpha and omega of the teacher's art, are things to which psychology cannot help us in the least.

(p. 18)

. . . The teacher's attitude towards the child, being concrete and ethical, is positively opposed to the psychological observer's, which is abstract and analytic. Although some of us may conjoin the attitudes successfully, in most of us they must conflict.

The worst thing that can happen to a good teacher is to get a bad conscience about her profession because she feels herself hopeless as a psychologist. Our teachers are overworked already. Everyone who adds a jot or tittle of unnecessary weight to their burden is a foe of education. A bad conscience increases the weight of every other burden; yet I know that child-study, and other pieces of psychology as well, have been productive of bad conscience in many a really innocent pædagogic breast. I should indeed be glad if this passing word from me might tend to dispel such a bad conscience, if any of you have it; for it is certainly one of those fruits of more or less systematic mystification of which I have already complained. The best teacher may be the poorest contributor of child-study material, and the best contributor may be the poorest teacher. No fact is more palpable than this.

So much for what seems the most reasonable general attitude of the teacher towards the subject which is to occupy our attention.

Conclusions to *A Pluralistic Universe*

Briefly, the facts I have in mind may all be described as experiences of an unexpected life succeeding upon death. . . . The phenomenon is that of new ranges of life succeeding on our most despairing moments. There are resources in us that naturalism with its literal and legal virtues never recks of, possibilities that take our breath away, of another kind of happiness and power, based on giving up our own will and letting something higher work for us, and these seem to show a world wider than either physics or philistine ethics can imagine.

(pp. 137–49)

At the close of my last lecture I referred to the existence of religious experiences of a specific nature. I must now explain just what I mean by such a claim. Briefly, the facts I have in mind may all be described as experiences of an unexpected life succeeding upon death. By this I don't mean immortality, or the death of the body. I mean the deathlike termination of certain mental processes within the individual's experience, processes that run to failure, and in some individuals, at least, eventuate in despair. Just as romantic love seems a comparatively recent literary invention, so these experiences of a life that supervenes upon despair seem to have played no great part in official theology till Luther's time; and possibly the best way to indicate their character will be to point to a certain contrast between the inner life of ourselves and of the ancient Greeks and Romans.

Mr. Chesterton, I think, says somewhere, that the Greeks and Romans, in all that concerned their moral life, were an extraordinarily solemn set of folks. The Athenians thought that the very gods must admire the rectitude of Phocion and Aristides; and those gentlemen themselves were apparently of much the same opinion. Cato's veracity was so impeccable that the extremest incredulity a Roman could express of anything was to say, "I would not believe it even if Cato had told me." Good was good, and bad was bad, for these people. Hypocrisy, which church-Christianity brought in, hardly existed; the naturalistic system held firm; its values showed no hollowness and brooked no irony. The individual, if virtuous enough, could meet all possible requirements. The pagan pride had never crumbled. Luther was the first moralist who broke with any effectiveness through the crust of all this naturalistic self-sufficiency, thinking (and possibly he was right) that Saint Paul had done it already. Religious experience of the Lutheran type brings all our naturalistic standards to bankruptcy. You are strong only by being weak, it shows. You cannot live on pride or self-sufficingness. There is a light in which all the naturally founded and currently accepted distinctions, excellences, and safeguards of our characters appear as utter childishness. Sincerely to give up one's conceit or hope of being good in one's own right is the only door to the universe's deeper reaches.

These deeper reaches are familiar to evangelical Christianity and to what is nowadays becoming known as "mind-cure" religion or "new thought." The phenomenon is that of new ranges of life succeeding on our most despairing moments. There are resources in us that naturalism with its literal and legal virtues never recks of, possibilities that take our breath away, of another kind of happiness and power, based on giving up our own will and letting something higher work for us, and these seem to show a world wider than either physics or philistine ethics can imagine. Here is a world in which all is well, *in spite* of certain forms of death, indeed *because* of certain forms of death—death of hope, death of strength, death of responsibility, of fear and worry, competency and desert, death of everything that paganism, naturalism, and legalism pin their faith on and tie their trust to.

Reason, operating on our other experiences, even our psychological experiences, would never have inferred these specifically religious experiences in advance of their actual coming. She could not suspect their existence, for they are discontinuous with the "natural" experiences they succeed upon and invert their values. But as they actually come and are given, creation widens to the view of their recipients. They suggest that our natural experience, our strictly moralistic and prudential experience, may be only a fragment of real human experience. They soften nature's outlines and open out the strangest possibilities and perspectives.

This is why it seems to me that the logical understanding, working in abstraction from such specifically religious experiences, will always omit something, and fail to reach completely adequate conclusions. Death and failure, it will always say, *are* death and failure simply, and can nevermore be one with life; so religious experience, peculiarly so called, needs, in my opinion, to be carefully considered and interpreted by everyone who aspires to reason out a more complete philosophy.

The sort of belief that religious experience of this type naturally engenders in those who have it is fully in accord with Fechner's theory of successively larger enveloping spheres of conscious life. To quote words which I have used elsewhere, the believer finds that the tenderer parts of his personal life are continuous with a *more* of the same quality which is operative in the universe outside of him and which he can keep in working touch with, and in a fashion get on board of and save himself, when all his lower being has gone to pieces in the wreck. In a word, the believer is continuous, to his own consciousness, at any rate, with a wider self from which saving experiences flow in. Those who have such experiences distinctly enough and often enough to live in the light of them remain quite unmoved by criticism, from whatever quarter it may come, be it academic or scientific, or be it merely the voice of logical common sense. They have had their vision and they *know*—that is enough—that we inhabit an invisible spiritual environment from which help comes, our soul being mysteriously one with a larger soul whose instruments we are.

One may therefore plead, I think, that Fechner's ideas are not without direct empirical verification. There is at any rate one side of life which would be easily explicable if those ideas were true, but of which there appears no clear explanation so long as we assume either with naturalism that human consciousness is the highest consciousness there is, or with dualistic theism that there is a higher mind in the cosmos, but that it is discontinuous with our own. It has always been a matter of surprise with me that philosophers of the absolute should have shown so little interest in this department of life, and so seldom put its phenomena in evidence, even when it seemed obvious that personal experience of some kind must have made their confidence in their own vision so strong. The logician's bias has always been too much with them. They have preferred the thinner to the thicker method, dialectical abstraction being so much more dignified and academic than the confused and unwholesome facts of personal biography.

In spite of rationalism's disdain for the particular, the personal, and the unwholesome, the drift of all the evidence we have seems to me to sweep us very strongly towards the belief in some form of superhuman life with which we may, unknown to ourselves, be co-conscious. We may be in the universe as dogs and cats are in our libraries, seeing the books and hearing the conversation, but having no inkling of the meaning of it all. The intellectualist objections to this fall away when the authority of intellectualist logic is undermined by criticism, and then the positive empirical evidence remains. The analogies with ordinary psychology, with certain facts of pathology, with those of psychical research, so called, and with those of religious experience, establish, when taken together, a decidedly *formidable* probability in favor of a general view of the world almost identical with Fechner's. The outlines of the superhuman consciousness thus made probable must remain, however, very vague, and the number of functionally distinct "selves" it comports and carries has to be left entirely problematic. It may be polytheistically or it may be monotheistically

conceived of. Fechner, with his distinct earth-soul func-
tioning as our guardian angel, seems to me clearly poly-
theistic; but the word "polytheism" usually gives offense,
so perhaps it is better not to use it. Only one thing is certain, and that is the result of our criticism of the absolute:
the only way to escape from the paradoxes and perplexi-
ties that a consistently thought-out monistic universe suf-
fers from as from a species of auto-intoxication—the
mystery of the "fall" namely, of reality lapsing into
appearance, truth into error, perfection into imperfection;
of evil, in short; the mystery of universal determinism, of
the block-universe eternal and without a history, etc.—
the only way of escape, I say, from all this is to be
frankly pluralistic and assume that the superhuman consciousness, however vast it may be, has itself an external
environment, and consequently is finite. Present day
monism carefully repudiates complicity with Spinosistic
monism. In that, it explains, the many get dissolved in
the one and lost, whereas in the improved idealistic form
they get preserved in all their manyness as the one's eternal object. The absolute itself is thus represented by
absolutists as having a pluralistic object. But if even the
absolute has to have a pluralistic vision, why should we
ourselves hesitate to be pluralists on our own sole
account? Why should we envelope our many with the
"one" that brings so much poison in its train?

The line of least resistance, then, as it seems to me,
both in theology and in philosophy, is to accept, along
with the super-human consciousness, the notion that it is
not all-embracing—the notion, in other words, that there
is a God, but that he is finite, either in power or knowledge, or in both at once. These, I need hardly tell you,
are the terms in which common men have usually
carried on their active commerce with God; and the

monistic perfections that make the notion of him so paradoxical practically and morally are the colder addition of
remote professorial minds operating *in distans* upon
conceptual substitutes for him alone.

Why cannot "experience" and "reason" meet on this
common ground? Why cannot they compromise? May not
the godlessness usually but needlessly associated with
the philosophy of immediate experience give way to a
theism now seen to follow directly from that experience
more widely taken? and may not rationalism, satisfied
with seeing her *a priori* proofs of God so effectively
replaced by empirical evidence, abate something of her
absolutist claims? Let God but have the least infinitesimal
other of any kind beside him, and empiricism and rationalism might strike hands in a lasting treaty of peace.
Both might then leave abstract thinness behind them, and
seek together, as scientific men seek, by using all the
analogies and data within reach, to build up the most
probable approximate idea of what the divine consciousness concretely may be like. I venture to beg the younger
Oxford idealists to consider seriously this alternative. Few
men are as qualified by their intellectual gifts as certain
of our present monistic philosophers to reap the harvests
that seem certain to anyone who, like Fechner and
Bergson, will leave the thinner for the thicker path.

Compromise and mediation are inseparable from the
pluralistic philosophy. Only monistic dogmatism can say
of any of its hypotheses, "It is either that or nothing; take
it or leave it just as it stands." The type of monism preva-
lent at Oxford has kept this steep and brittle attitude,
partly through the proverbial academic preference for
thin and elegant logical solutions, partly from a mistaken
notion that the only solidly grounded basis for religion
was along those lines. If Oxford men could be ignorant of

anything, it might almost seem that they had remained ignorant of the great empirical movement towards a pluralistic panpsychic view of the universe, into which our own generation has been drawn, and which threatens to short-circuit their methods entirely and become their religious rival unless they are willing to make themselves its allies. Yet, wedded as many of them seem to be to the logical machinery and technical apparatus of absolutism, I cannot but believe that their fidelity to the religious ideal in general is deeper still. Especially do I find it hard to believe that the more clerical adherents of the school would hold so fast to its particular machinery if only they could be made to think that religion could be secured in some other way. Let empiricism once become associated with religion, as hitherto, through some strange misunderstanding, it has been associated with irreligion, and I believe that a new era of religion as well as of philosophy will be ready to begin. That great awakening of a new popular interest in philosophy, which is so striking a phenomenon at the present day in all countries, is undoubtedly due in part to religious demands. As the authority of past tradition tends more and more to crumble, men naturally turn a wistful ear to the authority of reason or to the evidence of present fact. They will assuredly not be disappointed if they open their minds to what the thicker and more radical empiricism has to say. I fully believe that such an empiricism is a more natural ally than dialectics ever were, or can be, of the religious life. It is true that superstitions and wild-growing over-beliefs of all sorts will undoubtedly begin to abound if the notion of higher consciousness enveloping ours, of Fechnerian earth-souls and the like, grows orthodox and fashionable; still more will they superabound if science ever puts her approving stamp on the phenomena of which Frederic

Myers so earnestly advocated the scientific recognition, the phenomena of psychic research so called—and I myself firmly believe that most of these phenomena are rooted in reality. But ought one seriously to allow such a timid consideration as that to deter one from following the evident path of greatest religious promise? Since when, in this mixed world, was any good thing given us in purest outline and isolation? One of the chief characteristics of life is life's redundancy. The sole condition of our having *anything*, no matter what, is that we should have so much of it, that we are fortunate if we do not grow sick of the sight and sound of it altogether. Everything is smothered in the litter that is fated to accompany it. Without *too much* you cannot have *enough*, of anything. Lots of inferior books, lots of bad statues, lots of dull speeches, of tenth-rate men and women, as a condition of the few precious specimens in either kind being realized! The gold-dust comes to birth with the quartz-sand all around it, and this is as much a condition of religion as of any other excellent possession. There must be extrication; there must be competition for survival; but the clay matrix and the noble gem must first come into being unsifted. Once extricated, the gem can be examined separately, conceptualized, defined, and insulated. But this process of extrication cannot be short-circuited—or if it is, you get the thin inferior abstractions which we have seen, either the hollow unreal god of scholastic theology, or the unintelligible pantheistic monster, instead of the more living divine reality with which it appears certain that empirical methods tend to connect men in imagination.

Arrived at this point, I ask you to go back to my first lecture and remember, if you can, what I quoted there from your own Professor Jacks—what he said about the philosopher himself being taken up into the universe which he is accounting for. This is the Fechnerian as well as the Hegelian view, and thus our end rejoins harmoniously our beginning. Philosophies are intimate parts of the universe, they express something of its own thought of itself. A philosophy may indeed be a most momentous reaction of the universe upon itself. It may, as I said, possess and handle itself differently in consequence of us philosophers, with our theories, being here; it may trust itself or mistrust itself the more, and, by doing the one or the other, deserve more the trust or the mistrust. What mistrusts itself deserves mistrust.

This is the philosophy of humanism in the widest sense. Our philosophies swell the current of being, add their character to it. They are part of all that we have met, of all that makes us be. As a French philosopher says, "Nous sommes du réel dans le réel." Our thoughts determine our acts, and our acts redetermine the previous nature of the world.

Thus does foreignness get banished from our world, and far more so when we take the system of it pluralistically than when we take it monistically. We are indeed internal parts of God and not external creations, on any possible reading of the panpsychic system. Yet because God is not the absolute, but is himself a part when the system is conceived pluralistically, his functions can be taken as not wholly dissimilar to those of the other smaller parts—as similar to our functions consequently.

Having an environment, being in time, and working out a history just like ourselves, he escapes from the foreignness from all that is human, of the static timeless perfect absolute.

Remember that one of our troubles with that was its essential foreignness and monstrosity—there really is no other word for it than that. Its having the all-inclusive form gave to it an essentially heterogeneous *nature* from ourselves. And this great difference between absolutism and pluralism demands no difference in the universe's material content—it follows from a difference in the form alone. The all-form or monistic form makes the foreignness result, the each-form or pluralistic form leaves the intimacy undisturbed.

No matter what the content of the universe may be, if you only allow that it is *many* everywhere and always, that *nothing* real escapes from having an environment; so far from defeating its rationality, as the absolutists so unanimously pretend, you leave it in possession of the maximum amount of rationality practically attainable by our minds. Your relations with it, intellectual, emotional, and active, remain fluent and congruous with your own nature's chief demands.

It would be a pity if the word "rationality" were allowed to give us trouble here. It is one of those eulogistic words that both sides claim—for almost no one is willing to advertise his philosophy as a system of irrationality. But like most of the words which people used eulogistically, the word "rational" carries too many meanings. The most objective one is that of the older logic— the connexion between two things is rational when you can infer one from the other, mortal from Socrates, *e.g.*; and you can do that only when they have a quality in common. But this kind of rationality is just that logic of identity which all disciples of Hegel find insufficient. They supersede it by the higher rationality of negation and contradiction and make the notion vague again. Then you get the aesthetic or teleologic kinds of rationality, saying that whatever fits in any way, whatever is beautiful or good, whatever is purposive or gratifies desire, is rational in so far forth. Then again, according to

Hegel, whatever is "real" is rational. I myself said a while ago that whatever lets loose any action which we are fond of exerting seems rational. It would be better to give up the word 'rational' altogether than to get into a merely verbal fight about who has the best right to keep it.

Perhaps the words "foreignness" and "intimacy," which I put forward in my first lecture, express the contrast I insist on better than the words "rationality" and "irrationality"—let us stick to them, then. I now say that the notion of the "one" breeds foreignness and that of the "many" intimacy, for reasons which I have urged at only too great length, and with which, whether they convince you or not, I may suppose that you are now well acquainted. But what at bottom is meant by calling the universe many or by calling it one?

Pragmatically interpreted, pluralism or the doctrine that it is many means only that the sundry parts of reality *may be externally related*. Everything you can think of, however vast or inclusive, has on the pluralistic view a genuinely "external" environment of some sort or amount. Things are "with" one another in many ways, but nothing includes everything, or dominates over everything. The word "and" trails along after every sentence. Something always escapes. "Ever not quite" has to be said of the best attempts made anywhere in the universe at attaining all-inclusiveness. The pluralistic world is thus more like a federal republic than like an empire or a kingdom. However much may be collected, however much may report itself as present at any effective centre of consciousness or action, something else is self-governed and absent and unreduced to unity.

Monism, on the other hand, insists that when you come down to reality as such, to the reality of realities, everything is present to *everything* else in one vast instantaneous co-implicated completeness—nothing can in *any* sense, functional or substantial, be really absent from anything else, all things interpenetrate and telescope together in the great total conflux.

For pluralism, all that we are required to admit as the constitution of reality is what we ourselves find empirically realized in every minimum of finite life. Briefly it is this, that nothing real is absolutely simple, that every smallest bit of experience is a *multum in parvo* plurally related, that each relation is one aspect, character, or function, way of its being taken, or way of its taking something else; and that a bit of reality when actively engaged in one of these relations is not *by that very fact* engaged in all the other relations simultaneously. The relations are not *all* what the French call *solidaires* with one another. Without losing its identity a thing can either take up or drop another thing, like the log I spoke of, which by taking up new carriers and dropping old ones can travel anywhere with a light escort.

For monism, on the contrary, everything, whether we realize it or not, drags the whole universe along with itself and drops nothing. The log starts and arrives with all its carriers supporting it. If a thing were once disconnected, it could never be connected again, according to monism. The pragmatic difference between the two systems is thus a definite one. It is just thus, that if *a* is once out of sight of *b* or out of touch with it, or, more briefly, "out" of it at all, then, according to monism, it must always remain so, they can never get together; whereas pluralism admits that on another occasion they may work together, or in some way be connected again. Monism allows for no such things as "other occasions" in reality— in *real* or absolute reality, that is.

The difference I try to describe amounts, you see, to nothing more than the difference between what I formerly called the each-form and the all-form of reality. Pluralism lets things really exist in the each-form or distributively. Monism thinks that the all-form or collective-unit form is the only form that is rational. The all-form allows of no taking up and dropping of connexions, for in the all the parts are essentially and eternally co-implicated. In the each-form, on the contrary, a thing may be connected by intermediary things, with a thing with which it has no immediate or essential connexion. It is thus at all times in many possible connexions which are not necessarily actualized at the moment. They depend on which actual path of intermediation it may functionally strike into: the word "or" names a genuine reality. Thus, as I speak here, I may look ahead *or* to the right *or* to the left, and in either case the intervening space and air and ether enable me to see the faces of a different portion of this audience. My being here is independent of any one set of these faces.

If the each-form be the eternal form of reality no less than it is the form of temporal appearance, we still have a coherent world, and not an incarnate incoherence, as is charged by so many absolutists. Our "multiverse" still makes a "universe"; for every part, tho' it may not be in actual or immediate connexion, is nevertheless in some possible or mediated connexion, with every other part however remote, through the fact that each part hangs together with its very next neighbors in inextricable interfusion. The type of union, it is true, is different here from the monistic type of *alleinheit*. It is not a universal co-implication, or integration of all things *durcheinander*. It is what I call the strung-along type, the type of continuity, contiguity, or concatenation. If you prefer greek words, you may call it the synechistic type. At all events, you see that it forms a definitely conceivable alternative to the through-and-through unity of all things at once, which is the type opposed to it by monism. You see also that it stands or falls with the notion I have taken such pains to defend, of the through-and-through union of adjacent minima of experience, of the confluence of every passing moment of concretely felt experience with its immediately next neighbors. The recognition of this fact of coalescence of next with next in concrete experience, so that all the insulating cuts we make there are artificial products of the conceptualizing faculty, is what distinguishes the empiricism which I call "radical," from the bugaboo empiricism of the traditional rationalist critics, which (rightly or wrongly) is accused of chopping up experience into atomistic sensations, incapable of union with one another until a purely intellectual principle has swooped down upon them from on high and folded them in its own conjunctive categories.

Here, then, you have the plain alternative, and the full mystery of the difference between pluralism and monism, as clearly as I can set it forth on this occasion. It packs up into a nutshell:—Is the manyness-in-oneness that indubitably characterizes the world we inhabit, a property only of the absolute whole of things, so that you must postulate that one-enormous-whole indivisibly as the *prius* of there being any many at all—in other words, start with the rationalistic block-universe, entire, unmitigated, and complete?—or can the finite elements have their own aboriginal forms of manyness-in-oneness, and where they have no immediate oneness still be continued into one another by intermediary terms—each one of these terms being one with its next neighbors, and yet the total "oneness" never getting absolutely complete?

The alternative is definite. It seems to me, moreover, that the two horns of it make pragmatically different ethical appeals—at least they *may* do so, to certain individuals. But if you consider the pluralistic horn to be intrinsically irrational, self-contradictory, and absurd, I can now say no more in its defence. Having done what I could in my earlier lectures to break the edge of the intellectualistic *reductiones ad absurdum*, I must leave the issue in your hands. Whatever I may say, each of you will be sure to take pluralism or leave it, just as your own sense of rationality moves and inclines. The only thing I emphatically insist upon is that it is a fully coordinate hypothesis with monism. This world *may*, in the last resort, be a block-universe; but on the other hand it *may* be a universe only strung-along, not rounded in and closed. Reality *may* exist distributively just as it sensibly seems to, after all. On that possibility I do insist.

One's general vision of the probable usually decides such alternatives. They illustrate what I once wrote of as the "will to believe." In some of my lectures at Harvard I have spoken of what I call the "faith-ladder," as something quite different from the *sorites* of the logic-books, yet seeming to have an analogous form. I think you will quickly recognize in yourselves, as I describe it, the mental process to which I give this name.

A conception of the world arises in you somehow, no matter how. Is it true or not? you ask.

It *might* be true somewhere, you say, for it is not self-contradictory.

It *may* be true, you continue, even here and now.

It is *fit* to be true, it would be *well if it were true*, it *ought* to be true, you presently feel.

It *must* be true, something persuasive in you whispers next; and then—as a final result—

It shall be *held for true*, you decide; it *shall be* as if true, for *you*.

And your acting thus may in certain special cases be a means of making it securely true in the end.

Not one step in this process is logical, yet it is the way in which monists and pluralists alike espouse and hold fast to their visions. It is life exceeding logic, it is the practical reason for which the theoretic reason finds arguments after the conclusion is once there. In just this way do some of us hold to the unfinished pluralistic universe; in just this way do others hold to the timeless universe eternally complete.

Meanwhile the incompleteness of the pluralistic universe, thus assumed and held to as the most probable hypothesis, is also represented by the pluralistic philosophy as being self-reparative through us, as getting its disconnections remedied in part by our behavior. "We use what we are and have, to know; and what we know, to be and have still more."[1] Thus do philosophy and reality, theory and action, work in the same circle indefinitely.

I have now finished these poor lectures, and as you look back on them, they doubtless seem rambling and inconclusive enough. My only hope is that they may possibly have proved suggestive; and if indeed they have been suggestive of one point of method, I am almost willing to let all other suggestions go. That point is that *it is high time for the basis of discussion in these questions to be broadened and thickened up*. It is for that that I have brought in Fechner and Bergson, and descriptive psychology and religious experiences, and have ventured even to hint at psychical research and other wild beasts of the philosophic desert. Owing possibly to the fact that Plato and Aristotle, with their intellectualism, are the basis of philosophic study here, the Oxford brand of transcendentalism seems to me to have confined itself too exclusively to thin logical considerations, that would hold good in all conceivable worlds, worlds of an empirical constitution entirely different from ours. It is as if the actual peculiarities of the world that is were entirely irrelevant to the content of truth. But they cannot be irrelevant; and the philosophy of the future must imitate the sciences in taking them more and more elaborately into account. I urge some of the younger members of this learned audience to lay this hint to heart. If you can do so effectively, making still more concrete advances upon the path which Fechner and Bergson have so enticingly opened up, if you can gather philosophic conclusions of any kind, monistic or pluralistic, from the *particulars of life*, I will say, as I now do say, with the cheerfullest of hearts, "Ring out, ring out my mournful rhymes, but ring the fuller minstrel in."

---

[1] Blondel. *Annales de philosophie chrétienne*, June 1906, p. 241.

Index